Creative Cookery

Recipes from
The Barrett
Art
Center

Edited by Claudia Gorman with Ann Nihal

BARRETT
ART CENTER

Printed
September 2004

Edited by Claudia Gorman
with Ann Nihal

Printed by:

JUMBO
JACK'S COOKBOOKS
AUDUBON MEDIA CORPORATION
301 BROADWAY • AUDUBON IA 50025
1-800-798-2635

INTRODUCTION

Thomas Weeks Barrett, American regionalist and noted painter, was the first President of the Dutchess County Art Association, founded in 1936. It was his dream to convert his family home at 55 Noxon Street in Poughkeepsie into a community art center. In 1976, long after Barrett's death, his vision became a reality when his sister, Betty, bequeathed the family home to the Dutchess County Art Association. Since then, Barrett House has been a mainstay of the Hudson Valley arts community, serving as a gathering place for artists, giving them a space to show their work, as well as offering art classes, workshops and lectures. Studio space and darkroom rental is available, as well as a gallery that can be rented for solo exhibits. The Barrett Art Center provides an opportunity for individuals to learn, teach and grow. Openings of local and national shows are held throughout the calendar year. The artwork and photography included in this cookbook were contributed by B.A.C. members and friends, which is one of the unusual elements of this project.

Wonderful home cooked food has always been a part of Barrett House openings and other occasions. It has been our great pleasure to put together this collection of recipes, which demonstrates the artistic and culinary talent of the Barrett Art Center community. We hope you find joy both in trying these recipes and sampling the diverse dishes prepared using them. The Barrett Art Center annual chili dinner, held during the holiday season in December, is a much anticipated community event, which prompted the inclusion of a section in the cookbook devoted to chili recipes. We are fortunate to have a noted cookbook author, Nava Atlas, as a BAC member. She has been kind enough to share some of her recipes with us. In addition, you will find a chapter of recipes donated by chefs of local restaurants. We wish you happy cooking!

Claudia Gorman   Ann Nihol

Notes &
Recipes

Table of Contents

♥ – Indicates Heart-Healthy Recipes

FAVORITE RECIPES
FROM MY COOKBOOK

Recipe Name	Page Number

Breakfast,
Brunch and Lunch

Samuel Rein
Fruit on Striped Cloth
Gouache

Sandwich Fillings

Chicken and Sandwich Spread:
Add enough sandwich spread to finely chopped chicken to moisten.

Chicken and Nut:
Moisten chicken with mayonnaise. Add chopped nutmeats, lemon juice, and celery salt.

Chicken and Egg:
Combine 1 cup minced, cooked chicken, 2 hard-cooked egg yolks, 1 teaspoon chicken stock, 1 teaspoon lemon juice, and 1 teaspoon butter. Mix and spread.

Egg and Ham Salad:
Combine 6 hard-cooked eggs, diced; 1 cup cooked, diced ham; 6 sweet pickles, chopped; 1 cup chopped celery; 10 stuffed olives; and mayonnaise to moisten.

Date and Nut:
Combine 2/3 cup ground dates, 1/3 cup ground pecan meats, 1 1/2 tablespoons mayonnaise, and 1 tablespoon lemon juice. Mix and spread. Nice for rolled sandwiches.

Cream Cheese and Pineapple:
Combine cream cheese, crushed pineapple, and chopped nuts.

Ham Salad:
Combine 3/4 cup cooked, chopped ham; 1 tablespoon chopped onion; 1 hard-cooked egg, chopped; 1/4 cup chopped green peppers; and 1/4 cup mayonnaise.

Salmon and Nut:
Combine 1 cup flaked salmon, 3 tablespoons chopped nuts, 3 tablespoons minced celery, and 1/2 cup mayonnaise.

Tuna:
Combine tuna, chopped celery, walnuts and mayonnaise.

Tuna:
Combine tuna, crushed pineapple, chopped celery, and mayonnaise.

Chicken and Pineapple:
Combine 8-ounce can crushed pineapple, drained; 1 cup chopped, cooked chicken; 1/2 cup walnuts, chopped; and 1/2 cup cooked salad dressing. Spread between buttered slices of white bread. Remove crusts and cut each sandwich diagonally into quarters. Makes 4 dozen small sandwiches.

Pineapple and Cheese:
Combine 3 ounces cream cheese, 3 tablespoons mayonnaise, 1/2 cup chopped pecans, and 1/2 cup drained crushed pineapple. Mix and spread on crisp crackers or whole wheat bread.

Breakfast, Brunch and Lunch

♥ Frulatte Italiana a la Frencesco
(Smoothie)

1 banana
1 apple, strawberries or melon
1/2 c. soy milk (or milk)
1 c. fruit juice (any flavor)
1 tsp. vanilla
1 c. yogurt (any flavor)

2 scoops protein powder (opt.)
1 dash ginger (opt.)
1 dash cinnamon (opt.)
1 tsp. powdered Vitamin C
1/2 tsp. powdered Spirulina (opt.)

Blend until smooth. Drink cold or at room temperature.

Franc Palaia

Carol's Best Berry Griddlecakes

2 T. melted butter
1 egg
3/4 c. milk
1/3 c. oat flour
1/3 c. wheat flour
1/3 c. white flour
1/2 tsp. salt

1 T. sugar, to taste
2 1/2 tsp. baking powder
1/2 c. chopped nuts
1 c. frozen berries (I use 1/3 c. each
blueberries, raspberries,
cranberries--use fresh in season)

Beat melted butter, egg and milk lightly in a large mixing bowl. Mix the flours, baking powder, sugar, salt and nuts in a medium bowl and add them all at once to the first mixture, stirring just enough to dampen the flour. Add berry mixture and stir gently. If needed, add more milk to make the consistency loose enough to pour. Heat griddle to 350° and lightly butter (griddle is ready when water spits off it – the same is true on stovetop griddle). Pour batter on griddle in cd-sized cakes. That's it.

Note: I usually keep a large batch of the dry ingredients in a baggie, so all I have to do is mix up the wet ingredients and add the dry, kind of like a homemade biscuit mix. I use one cup of this for the above recipe.

Carol Zappelli

♥ Healthy, Dairy-Free Blueberry Pancakes

2 c. spelt, rice or soy flour	1 c. blueberries
1 c. vanilla soy yogurt	1 T. baking powder (opt.)
1 banana, mashed	1/2 tsp. nutmeg &/or cinnamon
2 scoops protein powder	1 c. soy or rice milk

Place 2 cups spelt, rice or soy flour in medium mixing bowl. Add 1 cup soy or rice milk, banana, protein powder, soy yogurt, nutmeg and/or cinnamon and blueberries. Mix thoroughly and pour onto hot griddle with heated canola oil or Smart Balance butter substitute.

These pancakes look like regular pancakes and are good for people who cannot digest dairy foods.

Eve D'Ambra

♥ Lactose-Free French Toast

(Wheat and Gluten-Free)

3 to 5 pieces spelt, sprontel or rice bread, sliced	2 eggs, or egg replacement
1/2 c. soy or rice milk	1/2 c. applesauce
3 bananas	1 tsp. cinnamon
	1 tsp. vanilla extract

Combine in bowl the eggs or egg replacement, applesauce, bananas, soy or rice milk, 1 teaspoon vanilla extract and cinnamon. Mix ingredients thoroughly and soak bread. Fry in pan with hot soy or canola oil. Brown both sides and serve with pure maple syrup and fresh blueberries, strawberries or melon.

French toast may be very moist; adjust amount of applesauce and/or bananas to your preference. Always try to use organic ingredients.

Franc Palaia

Onion and Corn Quiche

CRUST:
2 c. flour
3/4 tsp. salt

1/2 c. unsalted, chilled butter
3 T. ice water

FILLING:
4 eggs, well beaten
1 c. grated Swiss or Cheddar
  cheese, your choice
2 onions, sliced thin
4 c. cream, or 3 c. cream & 1 c. milk

1 (15 oz.) can organic corn, or frozen
  (2 to 3 ears corn, cooked & remove
  kernels from cob)
Salt & pepper, to taste
1 scallion, for top, chopped

Make crust for 9-inch pie pan by cutting chilled butter into flour and salt. Add water to crumbly; mix until a workable crust forms. Chill for 1/2 hour with plastic wrap.

Meanwhile, sauté onions until golden. Beat eggs and cream until well blended. Add salt and pepper to taste. Prepare (grate) cheese and set aside. Open can of corn and drain. Roll out chilled dough and make a nice, thin crust (cover with aluminum foil and place some dried beans on top to weight it down (this will keep crust flat). Bake for 15 minutes at 350°. Remove when goldish-tinted. Remove beans and foil; let sit.

For the remaining ingredients, put a layer of half the cheese on crust bottom. Pour in cream and eggs. Add corn and onions evenly. Don't forget the yummy onions go in the pan. Sprinkle the remaining cheese atop the ingredients. Sprinkle scallions on top of quiche. Bake for 30 minutes at 350°, until puffy, browned and solid. Enjoy!

You can use this basic crust/filling and add whatever other filling you'd like, for example: onions, olives, tomato slices, asparagus – anything.

K. Preyer

Egg Bagels

1 bagel, sliced in half horizontally   **Thin slices of Feta or Cheddar cheese**
1 egg   ·   **1 to 2 tsp. butter**

Beat egg in a container large enough to be able to soak bagel in egg. It takes a while for the bagel to soak up the egg. Use a frying pan large enough to hold both sides of bagel with a lid. Melt butter in pan and place bagel halves in with the crust-side facing up. Pour any extra egg into the hole of the bagel. Press bagels down with spatula. When first side is cooked, lower heat, flip bagels and place slices of cheese on top and cover with lid. Bagel will need to cook 3 to 5 minutes on each side, depending on how hot pan is.

This is a very modified version of French toast.

Claudia Gorman

Savory Brunch Bake

24 oz. frozen egg substitute, thawed,   **1/4 tsp. cumin**
** or 24 well-beaten eggs**   **1/8 tsp. cinnamon**
2 c. grated Mozzarella cheese   **1 sm. dash cayenne pepper**
1 to 1 1/2 c. cooked millet or brown   **Salt, to taste**
** rice**
1 to 1 1/2 c. mixed vegetables, raw
** or lightly-cooked & chopped**
** (scallions, onion, mushrooms,**
** baby spinach, or whatever you like)**

Mix all together. Pour into lightly-greased pan, about 9x13x2 inches. Bake at 350° for 30 to 35 minutes. Yield: 8 to 12 servings, depending on appetizers or whatever else you serve.

Preparation time: 15 to 30 minutes; baking time: 30 to 35 minutes.

Note: You can experiment with this by changing the cheeses, vegetables and spices. Dried bread, broken into pieces, can be substituted for the grain.   *Connye Eby*

♥ Egg Beaters Deluxe

This is a delicious treat for someone on a heart-healthy diet. The recipe is for a single portion. For multiple portions, amounts can be increased proportionately. Time is minimal – about 10 minutes, depending on skill of the chef.

1 egg white
1/3 c. Egg Beaters or comparable
   egg substitute
1/2 tsp. cottage cheese (preferably
   Friendship all natural 1% milk-
   fat cottage cheese)

Tabasco sauce
Freshly-ground black pepper
Olive oil

Add cottage cheese to egg white and beat thoroughly until egg white is frothy and cheese is completely dispersed.

In a separate bowl (or the measuring cup), add 2 or 3 drops Tabasco sauce and the pepper (to taste) to the Egg Beater. Add the seasoned Egg Beater to the egg white and mix thoroughly. Preheat a nonstick skillet and spray it with a light film of olive oil. Pour the egg mixture into the skillet and scramble it. Yield: 1 serving.

Variations: Slice 1 or 2 medium-sized white button mushrooms and sauté them in pan before adding egg mixture.

Wrap one slice of low-fat ham in 2 paper towels and microwave on HIGH HEAT for 30 seconds. Remove ham from paper and cut it into small pieces (1/2- to 3/4-inch squares). Sauté ham lightly before adding egg mixture.

Mince about 1 tablespoon onion or scallion and sauté before adding egg mixture.

Samuel Rein

My Granola Recipe

9 c. oats	2 1/2 c. brown sugar
4 c. oat bran	1 c. water
1 (6 oz.) bag sliced almonds	1 c. canola oil
3/4 c. soy powder	3 T. vanilla
1 c. honey	1 T. almond extract

Preheat oven to 300°. Mix everything together. Spread on cookie sheet and place in oven. Cook for 17 minutes; stir. Cook another 17 minutes until light brown. Remove from oven and stir while cooling.

Cynthia Dill

Crabmeat Brunch Bake

1 can Madam Brand crabmeat	Dash of salt
1 jar Kraft Old English cheese	Dash of pepper
spread, softened*	Dash of garlic powder
1 1/2 T. mayonnaise	Generous dash of celery salt
	1 pkg. English muffins

*Usually you can find this in the cheese section, near the cream cheese and pre-sliced American cheese. It's a little glass jar with a blue top.

Mix all ingredients together. Spread a layer over each split English muffin. Preheat oven to 325°. Place English muffins on a cookie sheet and bake until lightly browned (about 10 to 15 minutes).

Devaney Bennett

Black and White Bean Enchiladas

2 T. extra-virgin olive oil
1 c. chopped onion
1/2 c. orange or yellow bell
  peppers, diced
4 garlic cloves, minced
2 tsp. ground cumin
1 tsp. chili powder
1 (16 oz.) can crispy canned corn
  (or frozen, thawed)
1/2 c. canned vegetable broth

3 T. chopped fresh cilantro
1/8 tsp. salt
1/8 tsp. pepper
1 (16 oz.) can black beans, drained
1 (16 oz.) can white beans, drained
1 bag Mexican-style shredded
  cheese (I prefer Sargentino's)
8 (6") corn tortillas
Canola oil or cooking spray
1/4 c. sour cream, or more, to taste

Heat oil in a large, nonstick skillet over medium heat. Add onion, garlic and bell peppers; sauté for 3 minutes. Add cumin and chili powder; sauté for 1 minute. Stir in corn and the next 5 ingredients (corn through beans). Partially cover and cook 10 minutes, or until most of liquid evaporates. Remove from heat.

Warm tortillas according to package directions. Spoon about 1/3 cup bean mixture down center of each tortilla; roll up. Place enchiladas in a 9x13-inch baking dish with light coating of cooking spray or oil. Cover enchiladas with Mexican-style shredded cheese. Cover and bake at 350° for 20 minutes, or until thoroughly heated. Serve with sour cream and any one or all of my luscious salsa recipes. Yield: 4 servings.

MG Wells

Doug's Burnt-Cheese Quesadilla

6" corn tortillas (my wife has been known to eat 4 in 1 sitting)

Cheese (Jack or Cheddar, I prefer Cheddar), about 1/4 c. per quesadilla

Canned refried beans, they come spiced & plain – go with your preference or make fresh

Fresh cilantro, a few sprigs per

Diced onion (opt.)

Salsa, your favorite, or preferably make salsa fresca – take a trip to Molè Molè

Sour cream

Prepare on a large skillet or griddle-seasoned cast-iron is the best, although nonstick will do just fine. Slice cheese, dice onions and be ready!

Lightly rub cooking surface with oil, medium heat, until it just begins to smoke. Heat one side of a tortilla until it begins to show some signs of lightly cooking (usually a minute or so). Quickly lift and place sliced cheese directly on the cook surface – a little less than the size of the tortilla, and place the tortilla back down (cooked-side to the cheese).

Adjust heat if necessary to slow the process if it is going too fast, but it should be sizzling some.

Cook about another 2 minutes until the cheese sizzles and crusts and the tortilla can be lifted by spatula without sticking (when the cheese is cooked it will form a golden crust and easily release from the pan).

Flip over so the uncooked side of the tortilla is now on the pan and quickly spread some of the beans over the cheese, adding some of the diced onion, sour cream and a few sprigs of cilantro. Quickly fold in half and continue cooking on each side until tortilla reaches a slight crisp – or go longer if you prefer them crispier.

Plate them, top with salsa, and enjoy with your favorite Mexican beer, or a margarita, frozen or shaken.

A whole lot of taste in a tidy and quick meal! The cheese isn't really burnt so much as cooked; cheese when cooked, has much more depth of flavor than when just melted.

Doug Nobiletti

Breads
and Baked Goods

Margaret Crenson
Strawberries and Cream
Oil on Canvas

Baking Perfect Breads

Proportions

Biscuits .... To 1 cup flour use 1 1/4 teaspoons baking powder
Muffins .... To 1 cup flour use 1 1/2 teaspoons baking powder
Popovers .... To 1 cup flour use 1 1/4 teaspoons baking powder
Waffles .... To 1 cup flour use 1 1/4 teaspoons baking powder
Cake with fat .... To 1 cup flour use 1 teaspoon baking powder

Rules for Use of Leavening Agents

1. To 1 teaspoon soda use 2 1/4 teaspoons cream of tartar, or 2 cups freshly soured milk, or 1 cup molasses.
2. In simple flour mixtures, use 2 teaspoons baking powder to leaven 1 cup flour. Reduce this amount 1/2 teaspoon for each egg used.
3. To substitute soda and an acid for baking powder, divide the amount of baking powder by 4. Take that as your measure of and add the acid according to rule 1 above.

Proportions for Batters and Dough

Pour Batter .... To 1 cup liquid use 1 cup flour
Drop Batter .... To 1 cup liquid use 2 to 2 1/2 cups flour
Soft Dough .... To 1 cup liquid use 3 to 3 1/2 cups flour
Stiff Dough .... To 1 cup liquid use 4 cups flour

Hints for Baking

Kneading the dough for a half minute after mixing improves the texture of baking powder biscuits.

Use cooking or salad oil in waffles and hot cakes in the place of shortening. No extra pan or bowl to melt the shortening and no waiting.

When bread is baking, a small dish of water in the oven will help to keep the crust from getting hard.

Dip the spoon in hot water to measure shortening, butter, etc., the fat will slip out more easily.

Small amounts of leftover corn may be added to pancake batter for variety.

To make bread crumbs, use fine cutter of the food grinder and tie a large paper bag over the spout to prevent flying crumbs.

When you are doing any sort of baking, you get better results if you remember to preheat your cookie sheet, muffin tins or cake pans.

Oven Temperature Chart

Breads	Minutes	Temperature
Loaf	50-60	350°-400°
Rolls	20-30	400°-450°
Biscuits	12-15	400°-450°
Muffins	20-25	400°-450°
Popovers	30-40	425°-450°
Cornbread	25-30	400°-425°
Nut Bread	50-75	350°
Gingerbread	40-50	350°-370°

Breads and Baked Goods

♥ Cranberry Pumpkin Muffins

1 c. pumpkin (or sweet potato or
   winter squash), puréed
1/2 c. sugar
1/4 c. milk
2 eggs, or 4 whites
1/4 c. canola oil
1 c. whole wheat flour
1 c. white flour, or 1/2 c. soy flour,
   2 T. wheat germ + enough white
   flour to equal 1 c.

2 tsp. baking powder
1/4 tsp. salt
1/4 tsp. baking soda
1/4 tsp. cinnamon
1/4 tsp. cloves
1 c. fresh or frozen cranberries,
   coarsely chopped (I use a mini
   Cuisinart)

Preheat oven to 350°.

In a large bowl, mix together pumpkin, sugar, milk, eggs and canola oil.

In a separate bowl, combine flour, salt, baking soda, cinnamon and cloves. Add to pumpkin mixture. Stir until combined, and fold in cranberries. Grease muffin tin lightly, fill and bake for 30 minutes. Do not overcook. Alternately, fill a 9x9-inch baking pan and bake for 50 minutes. Yield: 12 muffins.

Nice for Thanksgiving! For a lower-fat version, replace oil with applesauce. You can add up to 1 cup sugar if you have a real sweet tooth!

Claudia Gorman

Blueberry Muffins

Blend:
1 stick butter
1 c. sugar

Mix (A):
2 eggs
1 tsp. vanilla
1/2 c. milk

Mix (B):
2 tsp. baking powder
1/2 tsp. salt
2 c. flour

2 c. blueberries

Add A and B in small alternate amounts to butter mix. Fold in 2 cups blueberries.

Grease muffin tin and the top of the pan. In a regular-size muffin tin, use 1/3 cup batter per muffin. Sprinkle top with sugar. Bake at 375° for 25 to 30 minutes. Cool on rack.

They are the best.

Vincent Scutellaro

Mini Popovers

1 1/4 c. flour
1/4 tsp. salt
3 lg. eggs
1 1/4 c. milk

2 T. unsalted butter, cut into even pieces
1 T. unsalted butter, melted

Oil or spray popover pan or small muffin pan. Preheat oven to 400° and set rack in middle of oven. Preheat popover pan. Blend flour, salt, eggs, milk and melted butter until it is the consistency of heavy cream. Batter can be made ahead and refrigerated, but use at room temperature.

Place 1 small piece of butter in each cup and melt it in pan. Fill each cup half-full with batter and bake 20 minutes. Reduce heat to 300° and continue baking for 15 to 20 minutes longer. Yield: 12 miniature popovers.

Batter can be used to make larger popovers.

Jackie Kingon

Scottish Oat Scones

2/3 c. melted butter or margarine	1/4 c. sugar
1/3 c. milk	1 T. baking powder
1 egg	1 tsp. cream of tartar
1 1/2 c. all-purpose flour	1/2 tsp. salt
1 1/4 c. quick Quaker Oats, uncooked	1/2 c. raisins or currants

Combine flour, oats, sugar, baking powder, cream of tartar and salt. Add butter, milk and egg; mix until just moistened. Stir in raisins. Shape dough to form ball. Pat out on lightly-floured surface to form 8-inch circle. Cut into 8 to 12 wedges. Bake on greased cookie sheet at 425° for 12 to 15 minutes, or until light golden brown. Yield: 8 to 12 scones.

Shirley Karnes

Overnight Caramel Rolls

1 pkg. frozen bread dough* thawed & formed into little dough balls, about the size of a golf ball	1/2 c. brown sugar
	1/4 c. butter
	3/4 pkg. regular butterscotch pudding mix
1 c. chopped pecans	3/4 tsp. cinnamon

Generously grease a tube or bundt pan. Layer the dough balls in the bottom of the pan in a circle. Sprinkle pudding over dough, then sprinkle nuts over that. Mix butter, cinnamon and brown sugar; heat to just boiling. Pour this over dough. Cover with buttered plastic wrap or waxed paper and place in a cold oven overnight.

The next morning, remove the pan from the oven and remove the plastic or waxed paper. Preheat oven to 350° and bake for 25 to 30 minutes.

After removing from oven, invert immediately onto serving plate. Let sit a minute or two, and then remove the pan. Yummy!

*Can also use frozen roll dough.

Carol Jarvis

Apricot Bread

1 c. apricots, chopped
1 c. boiling water
1 c. orange juice
1 c. raisins
2 tsp. baking soda
1 stick margarine

2 c. sugar
2 eggs
4 c. flour
1 1/2 tsp. salt
1 c. chopped nuts

Preheat oven to 350°. Grease 2 (46-ounce) coffee cans.

Combine apricots, boiling water, orange juice, raisins and baking soda in a bowl. In another large bowl, stir together margarine, sugar and eggs. Add flour and salt. Stir. Add apricot mixture and chopped nuts. Stir until combined. Fill 2 coffee cans half-full and bake at 350° for 1 to 1 1/4 hours. Let bread cool a little, then gently roll the can back and forth to get the bread out.

Margot Finn

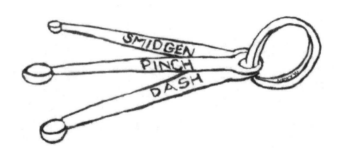

Golden Cornbread

1 c. sifted all-purpose flour
1/4 c. sugar
5 tsp. baking powder
3/4 tsp. salt

1 c. yellow cornmeal
2 eggs
1 c. milk
1/4 c. soft butter

Sift together flour, sugar, baking powder and salt. Stir in cornmeal.

In a separate bowl, beat eggs. Add milk and butter. Add all at one time to cornmeal mixture. Stir with fork only until flour is moistened. Even if batter is lumpy, do not stir any more. Pour into well-greased 8- or 9-inch square pan. Bake at 425° for 20 to 25 minutes, or until done. Cut into squares and serve hot with butter and honey. Yield: 9 servings.

Ruth Dill

Sour Cream Coffeecake

1/4 lb. butter, unsalted
1 c. sugar
2 eggs
2 c. flour
1 tsp. baking soda
1 tsp. baking powder

1/4 tsp. salt
1/2 pt. sour cream
1 tsp. almond extract
1/2 c. chopped pecans or walnuts
1/2 c. sugar
2 tsp. cinnamon

Preheat oven to 350°. Beat until fluffy, the butter, 1 cup sugar and eggs (one at a time). Sift dry ingredients (flour, baking soda, baking powder and salt). Blend in flour mixture to butter mix and add sour cream with almond extract.

Pour half the batter into a buttered and floured cake or tube pan. Sprinkle half of the mixed nuts, sugar and cinnamon in middle. Pour the rest of batter over nut mixture. Sprinkle remaining nut mixture on top of batter. Bake for 40 to 45 minutes at 350°. Watch, do not overbake.

Cool, cut and enjoy!

K. Preyer

Overnight Coffeecake

2/3 c. margarine or butter
1 c. brown sugar
1/2 c. white sugar
2 beaten eggs
1/2 tsp. salt
1/2 tsp. nutmeg

1 c. buttermilk
2 c. flour
1 tsp. baking powder
1 tsp. baking soda
1/2 c. walnuts, chopped

Cream margarine with half of the brown sugar (1/2 cup) and the white sugar; add beaten eggs and buttermilk.

In a separate bowl, combine the dry ingredients, except the nutmeg and walnuts; add to the creamed mixture. Pour into a 9x13-inch pan. Combine the walnuts, nutmeg and remaining brown sugar, and sprinkle this mixture on top. Cover with plastic wrap and refrigerate overnight.

Can be baked right away, or the next morning, in a 350° oven for 30 to 35 minutes.

Great when you have overnight guests.

Carol Jarvis

Biscotti from Greve, Italy

2 c. unbleached flour
1 c. sugar
1 tsp. baking soda
1/4 tsp. salt
2 lg. whole eggs
1 lg. egg yolk

1 tsp. vanilla
1 T. freshly-grated orange zest
1 1/2 c. whole almonds, toasted
   lightly & chopped coarse
1 lg. egg & 1 tsp. water, beaten
   together (egg wash)

Blend flour, sugar, baking soda and salt.

In a small bowl, whisk the whole eggs, the yolk, vanilla and zest. Then add to flour mixture, mix and stir in almonds. Turn dough out onto a lightly-floured surface, knead it and divide in half. With floured hands, form each piece into a flatish log (12 inches long, 2 inches wide). Place on buttered and floured baking sheet and brush logs with an egg wash. Bake logs in 300° oven for 50 minutes. Let them cool for 10 minutes on a board, cut the logs crosswise on the diagonal into 1/2-inch slices. Bake both sides of the biscotti for 15 minutes at 300°. Cool and store. Yield: 48 biscotti.

Ann Lawrance Morse

Steve's Wholesome Banana-Nut Loaf

1/2 c. oil
3/4 c. brown sugar
2 eggs
3 very-ripe bananas
1 c. unbleached all-purpose flour
1/2 c. whole wheat flour
1/2 c. flaxseed meal
1/2 tsp. salt
3 T. skim milk
1/2 tsp. vanilla
1/2 c. (or more) walnuts, chopped

Beat oil, sugar, eggs and bananas until well blended. Add flour, baking soda, baking powder and salt, mixing only until moistened. Add skim milk, vanilla and walnuts; mix thoroughly. Pour into a lightly-oiled 5x9-inch loaf pan. Bake at 350° for 1 hour, or check until done. Cool before removing from pan. Yield: 1 loaf.
Preparation time: 15 minutes; baking time: 1 hour.
Can freeze.

Stephen H. Aronson

♥ Sharyn's Low-Fat Apple Pie Coffeecake

2 eggs
1 T. vegetable oil
1/4 tsp. vanilla
3/4 c. sugar
1/2 c. flour
1/2 c. oatmeal
2 tsp. baking powder
1/2 tsp. cinnamon
1/4 tsp. nutmeg
1/4 tsp. salt
2 c. peeled & sliced apples
1 T. raw sugar, for top

Grease 10-inch pie pan.
In a medium bowl, combine the eggs, oil, vanilla and sugar; beat with a wooden spoon until thick, about 1 minute. Add flour and oatmeal, baking powder, cinnamon, nutmeg and salt. Beat vigorously until batter is smooth, about 1 minute. Fold in apples and mix until coated (it will look like too many apples for batter, but it's not). Scrape batter into prepared pan and smooth out into an even layer. Sprinkle top with sugar. Bake for 30 to 35 minutes, until center is firm. A cake tester should come out clean. Serve warm and cut into wedges from pan.

Sharyn Cadogan

HOW TO SLICE ITALIAN BREAD

INGREDIENTS: 1 LOAF ITALIAN BREAD (UNCUT)
EQUIPMENT: BAND SAW, SAFETY GOGGLES,
RESPIRATOR, CHEF'S HAT (OPTIONAL)

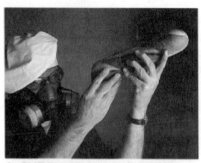

1. CHECK GRAIN PATTERN

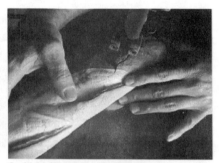

2. HOLD BREAD FIRMLY

3. SLIDE BREAD THRU BLADE

CHEF JEFF DOESN'T KNOW

"HOW I GOT ALONG WITHOUT THIS HANDY LITTLE GOURMET APPLIANCE" (AVAILABLE AT YOUR LOCAL HARDWARE SUPPLY STORE)

4. A FANCY CUT READY TO EAT.... BON APPETIT!

Heavenly Hungarian Fennel Bread

4 to 5 c. unsifted flour
2 tsp. sugar
2 tsp. salt
1 heaping T. fennel seeds
2 pkg. yeast

2 T. softened butter or melted margarine
1 3/4 c. very hot tap water
Cornmeal
1 egg yolk
2 tsp. cream or milk

Thoroughly mix 1 1/2 cups flour, sugar, salt, half the fennel seeds and yeast in a large bowl. Add butter. Gradually add very hot tap water to dry ingredients and beat for 2 minutes at medium speed with electric mixer, or by hand. Add 1/2 cup flour, or enough to make thick batter and beat vigorously for another 2 minutes. Stir in enough additional flour to make a soft dough; turn out on a lightly-floured board and knead until dough is smooth and elastic, about 8 minutes. Place in buttered bowl and cover; let stand to rise in a warm place until doubled in bulk, about 30 minutes. Punch down. Turn out on lightly-floured board. Divide in half and form into round balls. Place 1 at each end of cookie sheet that has been well-buttered and sprinkled with cornmeal. Cover and let rise again until double in bulk, about another 30 minutes.

Beat egg yolk and cream (or milk) together and brush over loaves. Sprinkle remaining fennel seeds on loaves. Bake in 400° oven for about 30 minutes, or until done. Remove loaves from baking sheet and cool on rack(s).

Samuel Rein

Sourdough Garlic Onion Bread

2 (1 lb.) loaves round sourdough
   bread, unsliced
3 sticks unsalted butter (margarine),
   room temp.
1/2 c. parsley, finely chopped
1/2 c. scallions, finely minced
1 tsp. salt

1 tsp. basil, dried
1 tsp. thyme, dried
1 tsp. oregano, dried
1/2 tsp. rosemary, dried
4 med. cloves garlic, peeled &
   crushed
6 T. Parmesan cheese, grated

Preheat oven to 325°. Trim the crust from the tops and sides of both loaves of bread. Cut diagonal slices, 2 inches thick across bread, without cutting through the bottoms of breads. Cut slices in opposite direction, again 2 inches thick, forming diamond shapes.

In mixing bowl or food processor with metal blade, combine butter, parsley, scallions, salt, basil, thyme, oregano, rosemary and garlic, and then blend.

Spread butter or margarine mixture between all the cuts and over top and sides of the loaves. Sprinkle the Parmesan cheese on the tops of loaves and then bake for approximately 35 to 40 minutes, until golden brown. Yield: 8 servings.

Note: May be wrapped in foil and refrigerated overnight or frozen ahead of time. Before serving, place on baking sheet and bring to room temperature. Heat at 300° for 10 minutes. Leftovers can be wrapped in foil and reheated in low oven.

Mildred Cohen

Appetizers

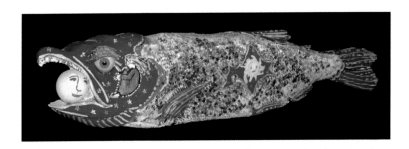

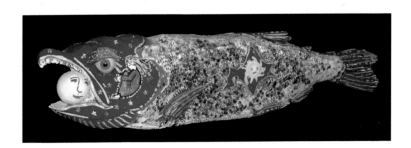

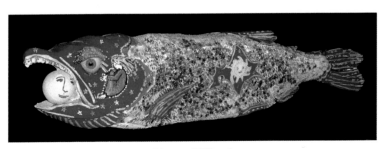

Nancy Willard
Fish
Mixed Media

Seasoning Guide

Get acquainted with spices and herbs. Add in small amounts, 1/4 teaspoon for each 4 servings. Taste before adding more. Crush dried herbs or snip fresh herbs before using. If substituting fresh for dried, use 3 times more fresh herbs.

Appetizers, Soups

STUFFED CELERY: Mix caraway seed with cream cheese; fill celery. Dash with paprika.

TOMATO COCKTAIL: Add 1/4 teaspoon dried basil per cup.

CHICKEN SOUP: Add a dash of rosemary, tarragon, or nutmeg. Sprinkle paprika atop for color.

CLAM CHOWDER: Add a dash of caraway seed, sage, or thyme.

CONSOMMÉ: Dash in basil, marjoram, savory, or tarragon.

MUSHROOM SOUP: Season with curry, oregano, or marjoram.

ONION SOUP: Add marjoram.

OYSTER STEW: Lightly add cayenne, mace, or marjoram.

POTATO SOUP: Dash with mustard or basil. Top with snipped chives or parsley.

SPLIT-PEA SOUP: Add dash basil, chili powder, or rosemary.

TOMATO SOUP: Dash in basil, dill, oregano, sage, or tarragon.

VEGETABLE SOUP: Try allspice, oregano, sage, or thyme.

Breads, Pasta

BISCUITS: Add caraway seed, thyme, or savory to flour. Serve with meat.

BREAD: Make each loaf a surprise by adding caraway seed, cardamom, or poppy seed.

COFFEE CAKE: Mix crushed anise in batter. For variety, sprinkle cinnamon-sugar mixture atop or add poppy seed filling.

CORNBREAD: Add poultry seasoning or caraway seed to dry ingredients. Be adventuresome; add 1/2 teaspoon rosemary to batter.

CROUTONS: Toss toast cubes in melted butter seasoned with basil, marjoram, or onion salt.

DOUGHNUTS: Add mace or nutmeg to dry ingredients. After frying, roll in cinnamon-sugar.

DUMPLINGS: Add thyme or parsley (fresh or flakes) to batter.

MUFFINS: Blueberry -- add dash of nutmeg to dry ingredients. Season plain muffins with caraway or cinnamon.

NOODLES: Butter, then sprinkle with poppy seed.

ROLLS: Add caraway seed. Or, sprinkle with sesame seed.

SPAGHETTI: Toss with butter, Parmesan, and snipped chives.

Eggs, Cheese

BAKED EGGS: Sprinkle dash of thyme or paprika over the top.

CREAMED EGGS: Add mace.

DEVILED EGGS: Add celery seed, cumin, mustard, savory, chili powder, or curry powder.

OMELET: Try with dash of marjoram or rosemary (go easy!).

SCRAMBLED EGGS: Sprinkle lightly with basil, thyme, rosemary, or marjoram. Add seasoning near the end of cooking.

SOUFFLÉ: Add 1/4 teaspoon marjoram to 4-egg soufflé. To cheese soufflé, add basil or savory.

CHEESE CASSEROLES: Spark with dash sage or marjoram.

CHEESE FONDUE: Try adding a dash of basil or nutmeg.

CHEESE RAREBIT: Try with mace or mustard.

CHEESE SAUCE: Add mustard or a dash of marjoram or thyme.

CHEESE SPREAD: Blend sage, caraway seed, thyme, or celery seed into melted processed cheese.

COTTAGE CHEESE: Blend in chives or a dash of sage, caraway seed, dill, anise or cumin. Prepare several hours ahead of time.

Appetizers

Why Cook?!

Negroni

1 1/2 oz. gin   1 1/2 oz. sweet vermouth
1 1/2 oz. campari

Combine ingredients in shaker of ice. Strain and pour into chilled martini glass. Garnish with lemon zest.

Chocolate Mint Martini

1 oz. vodka   1/2 oz. white creme de cacao
1/2 oz. white creme de menthe

Combine ingredients in shaker filled with ice. Strain and pour into chilled martini glass.

Vodka Martini

1 1/2 oz. vodka   1 olive or twist of lemon peel
3/4 oz. dry vermouth

Combine ingredients in shaker filled with ice. Strain and pour into chilled martini glass.

Hummus
(Garbanzo Bean Dip)

4 to 5 T. tahini sesame paste
Juice of 2 to 3 lemons
1 med. clove garlic, crushed
1/2 tsp. salt

1/8 c. juice from canned garbanzo
   beans (chickpeas)
1 (16 oz.) can chickpeas

Put above ingredients in blender. Serve on plate garnished with chopped parsley and tomato wedges. Serve at room temperature with pita or French bread, or on crackers.

L. Clarke

♥ Mushroom Caviar

1 T. olive oil
4 scallions, minced
1/2 lb. portobello mushrooms, cut
   into 1/2" cubes
6 cloves garlic, roughly chopped

1/2 tsp. fresh thyme, chopped
2 tsp. lemon juice
4 tsp. balsamic vinegar
1/4 tsp. freshly-ground black pepper

In a large saucepan, heat 1 teaspoon olive oil and sauté scallions until tender; set aside. Heat remaining oil and sauté mushrooms, garlic and thyme until mushrooms and garlic are tender. Do not overcrowd pan or mushrooms will poach rather than sauté. Transfer mushrooms and scallions to food processor. Using pulse button, process until coarsely chopped (this means that you are chopping again those ingredients you chopped before you began the recipe). Return to saucepan. Add lemon juice, vinegar and pepper; sauté over medium-high heat until liquid has evaporated. When you are all done, this should be just a little more coarse than a paste. Serve in small crock or dish as a spread for toast. Yield: about 16 servings.

Maryjane

Irene Weinberg's Gefilte Fish

7 lb. whitefish	4 grated onions
3 lb. pike	8 grated carrots
5 sliced carrots	Salt & pepper, to taste
3 sliced onions	1 tsp. sugar
Salt & pepper, to taste	1/2 to 1 c. water
7 eggs	

Fillet whitefish and pike; grind it. After filleting, you should have approximately 5 pounds ground fish; set aside. Save bones and heads for cooking. Arrange bones, heads and skin in large pot. Cover bones, etc., with sliced carrots and onions, salt and pepper. Add water to cover the above mixture, plus some extra.

Bring above ingredients to a boil. Continue boiling (cover pot) for 30 minutes.

Meanwhile, mix together eggs, grated onion, carrots, salt, pepper, sugar and 1/2 cup water. Mix this thoroughly with the ground fish. You might need a little more water to make the mixture into a consistency so that you can form it into balls. Make medium-sized gefilte fish balls.

Add fish balls to boiled broth; lower heat after all ingredients return to a boil. Cook for 30 minutes. Uncover pot and cook on medium heat for approximately 2 hours.

Cheryl Schneider

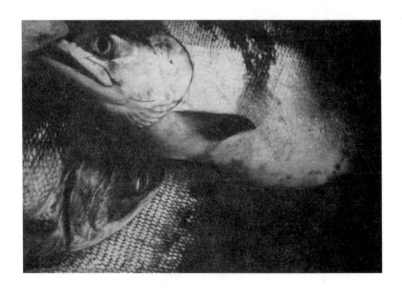

Hot Cheese Dip

1 c. Hellmann's mayonnaise
1 c. shredded Cheddar cheese

1 onion, chopped fine

Mix well. Put in a shallow dish. Bake at 400° for 20 minutes.

Diane Sipos

Soups
and Salads

Claudia Gorman
Banana Tree
Hand Colored Emulsion Transfer on Paper

Hints for Salads

- When buying grapefruit, judge it by its weight. The heavier ones are juicier.
- Add 1/4 teaspoon soda to cranberries while cooking and they will not require as much sugar.
- Frosted Grapes: Beat 2 egg whites and 2 tablespoons water slightly. Dip small clusters of grapes into the mixture. Sprinkle with granulated sugar. Dry on waxed paper.
- Lemons that are heated before squeezing will give almost twice the quantity of juice.
- Lemon juice on cut bananas will keep them from darkening.
- Grease the salad mold with salad dressing, mayonnaise or salad oil and it will help the salad slip out easily.
- Save sweet pickle juice. Store it in the refrigerator and use small amounts to thin dressings for salads.
- Soak hard-cooked eggs in beet pickle juice for an interesting taste and colorful garnish.
- To make a hard-cooked egg flower: Cut white from the small end of the egg about 3/4 of the way down, petal fashion, being careful not to cut yolk. When spread apart, these white petals should show yolk as a round ball, daisy fashion. Slice green pepper for leaves. Nice for potato salad.
- Marshmallows will cut easily if the blades of the scissors are buttered.
- Try putting marshmallows in the refrigerator and they won't stick to the scissors.
- Perk up soggy lettuce by adding lemon juice to a bowl of cold water and soaking it for an hour in the refrigerator.
- The darker, outer leaves of lettuce are higher in calcium, iron and Vitamin A.
- Do not add salt to a lettuce salad until just before serving; salt makes the lettuce wilt and become tough.
- Toss salads well so you can use less dressing which is healthier.
- Prepare ingredients such as greens, chopped onions, celery, carrots and radishes ahead of time. Store in separate airtight containers for quick use in a tossed salad.
- When you will be doing extra cooking, keep shredded cheese, bread crumbs, and chopped onion on hand for use in salads, casseroles and vegetables.
- Before grating cheese, brush vegetable oil on the grater and it will clean easier.
- Remove the tops of carrots before storing. Tops absorb moisture and nutrients from the carrots.
- It is easy to remove the white membrane from oranges - for fancy desserts or salads - by soaking them in boiling water for 5 minutes before you peel them.
- Lemon Jello, dissolved in 2 cups of hot apricot nectar with 1 teaspoon of grated lemon added for zip, makes a perfect base for jelled fruit salad.

Soups & Salads

♥ Chilled Minted Cucumber Honeydew Soup

Can be prepared in 45 minutes or less, but requires additional unattended time.

1 English cucumber	**1/4 c. fresh mint leaves**
2 c. honeydew pieces, from about	**2 T. fresh lime juice**
1/4 med. melon	**4 fresh mint leaves, for garnish**
8 oz. plain nonfat yogurt	

Cut cucumber into 1-inch pieces. In a bowl, combine cucumber and honeydew pieces, yogurt, mint leaves and lime juice.

In a blender, purée mixture in batches 30 seconds, pouring mixture as puréed through a sieve into a bowl, and season soup with salt and pepper. Chill soup, covered, at least 2 hours and up to 6. Serve soup garnished with mint. Yield: 5 cups (4 servings).

Each serving about 73.5 calories and 0.28 gm fat (3% calories from fat).

Leila Meehan

*"Friends are like melons, Shall I tell you why?
To find one good, You must a hundred try."*
Claude Mermel, 1600

♥ Tomatillo-Zucchini Soup

1 T. cooking oil
1 lg. onion, chopped coarsely
6 cloves garlic, chopped coarsely
2 green or red (or combination) peppers, seeded & chopped coarsely
1 or 2 chili peppers or scotch bonnet peppers

1 lg. or 2 med. zucchini, chopped coarsely
10 to 12 sm. tomatillos, peeled & chopped, or cut into wedges
5 to 6 c. chicken or vegetable broth
1 T. fresh cilantro, chopped
1 to 2 T. lime juice
1 T. fresh cilantro leaves (whole for garnish)

OPTIONAL SIDES:
Shredded Mexican-style cheeses

Sour cream
Corn tortillas

Preheat soup pot. When hot, add oil, then onion and garlic; cook over medium heat, stirring until onion is soft.

Add peppers and cook, stirring 1 minute more. Add zucchini and tomatillos and continue to cook, stirring, until coated and heated through. Add broth and chopped cilantro and bring to a boil.

Reduce heat and simmer, covered, until zucchini is soft, about 20 minutes. Remove from heat and allow to cool some. When it is cool enough, purée the soup in a food processor or blender (you may have to do this in batches). Return to low heat; stir in lime juice. Bring soup back to hot over low heat. Serve with optional sides, if desired. Yield: 4 dinner servings, or 6 appetizer servings.

Note: People who don't or can't eat peppers can leave them out. Tomatillos have a peppery taste, so the flavor will still be there, just less pronounced. Make up for the missing bulk with more tomatillos. Those who don't like hot peppers can eliminate them from the recipe.

Paula Poons

"An idealist is one who, on noticing that a rose smells better than a cabbage, concludes that it will also make a better soup."
(H.L. Mencken 1880-1956)

♥ Curried Lentil-Vegetable Soup Extraordinaire

2 c. lentils
7 c. purified water
2 stalks celery
3 carrots
1 c. fresh spinach
2 T. Biryani paste (Indian curry paste)
1 can Ro-Tel mild tomatoes & chilies
  (sold in Hispanic grocery stores)
1/2 c. chopped green peppers

1/2 c. red peppers
1 c. onions
1 "strip" kombu or wakame
  (seaweed)
3 T. chopped, fresh garlic
4 T. Bragg's liquid aminos
  (unfermented soy sauce)
2 T. Lawry's seasoned salt, or to taste

Put all ingredients in a crock-pot and cook on low heat for 7 to 8 hours, or until the lentils are tender. Yield: 4 servings.

Serve with whole grain bread or healthy crackers and a rainbow salad.

This is a great dish to leave cooking while you go to work, and when you return, your home welcomes you with the delightful scent of homemade soup.

This is a wonderful crock-pot recipe that I created for my Asian Nutrition class. It has such great flavor!

Yvonne Lewis

♥ Potato, Cheese and Green Chili Soup

5 med. potatoes, peeled & diced
5 c. prepared vegetable stock, or water with 2 vegetable bouillon cubes
1 T. light olive oil
1 lg. onion, chopped
2 to 3 cloves garlic, crushed or minced
1 lg. green bell pepper, finely chopped

1 c. chopped ripe tomatoes
1 c. cooked fresh or thawed, frozen corn kernels
1 (4 oz.) can chopped mild green chilies
1 tsp. chili powder
8 oz. organic Cheddar or Cheddar-style soy cheese, grated
Salt & freshly-ground pepper, to taste

Place the potato dice in a soup pot and cover with the stock or water. Bring to a simmer, then simmer gently, covered, until the potatoes are just tender, about 15 minutes.

Meanwhile, heat the oil in a small skillet. Sauté the onion over medium heat until it is translucent. Add the garlic and green pepper; sauté until the mixture begins to brown lightly.

Remove half of the potatoes from their cooking liquid with a slotted spoon and place them in a shallow bowl. Mash then well, then stir back into the soup pot, followed by the onion-bell pepper mixture. Add the tomatoes, corn, green chilies and chili powder. Add additional water if the soup is too dense. Stir together; return to a simmer, then simmer gently for 20 minutes. Sprinkle in the grated cheese, a little at a time, stirring it until it is fairly well melted each time (soy cheese may not melt as completely). Season to taste with salt and pepper and allow the soup to simmer over very low heat, stirring frequently, for another 5 minutes.

Serve at once, or let stand for an hour or so before serving. Heat through as needed and adjust the consistency with more water if the soup becomes too thick. Yield: 6 to 8 servings.

This flavorful soup is a contemporary classic from the American Southwest. A great soup to make in the early fall, while fresh corn and tomatoes are still available.

Adapted from "Vegetarian Soups for All-Seasons" by **Nava Atlas**.

"Eat soup first and eat it last,
and live till a hundred years past"
(French Proverb)

Squash Soup

1 sm. to med. pumpkin (pulp)	1/4 tsp. cinnamon
3 lg. carrots	Dash of nutmeg
1 apple	1/2 tsp. ginger (fresh)
1 potato	2 T. brown sugar
2 1/2 c. vegetable broth	Salt, to taste
3 T. margarine	Milk, enough to allow easy blending

Cook pumpkin until soft, then blend smooth, all the ingredients. Add milk to blender as needed.

Try this recipe with any winter squash.   *Cynthia Dill*

Cream of Mushroom Soup

12 oz. fresh button mushrooms	Pinch of nutmeg
1 sm. onion, peeled & finely chopped	Salt & pepper
2 T. butter	3 to 4 mushroom caps, thinly sliced,
1 T. flour	for garnish
3 3/4 c. good chicken stock	Chopped parsley, for garnish
1 3/4 c. milk	3 T. heavy cream, for garnish

Wipe and trim the mushrooms and chop them finely, reserving 3 to 4 for garnish. Using a large, heavy-based pan, sauté the onion and mushrooms in the butter for 4 to 5 minutes. Stir in the flour and cook for a further minute. Take the pan off the heat, add the stock and milk; stir well. Return the pan to medium heat and cook, stirring continuously, until the soup thickens. Add the nutmeg, season to taste and allow the soup to simmer, covered, for about 15 minutes. Serve in warmed bowls, garnished with a swirl of cream, mushroom slices and chopped parsley.

James Ransome

Cabbage Soup

2 onions, diced
1 sm. head cabbage, sliced
1 lb. meat (lean chopped beef or
 turkey)
2 lg. cans tomatoes

Ginger powder
Garlic powder
Red pepper
1 T. sugar

Sauté onion, cabbage and meat or turkey in a large pot.
Add tomatoes, spices to taste and sugar. Simmer 2 to 3 hours. Add lemon juice to taste at end of cooking.   *Enid Watsky*

Thai Soba Soup

1/2 lb. (or 16) shrimp
1 bunch broccoli (sm. bunch florets)
1 med. onion, chopped
3 to 4 cloves garlic, chopped
Several mint leaves
1/4 c. arrowroot or flour

12 oz. soba noodles
1/2 tsp. ginger
1 tsp. orange peel, shaved
1 tsp. coriander
1 bunch cilantro
2 T. peanut oil

In a medium saucepan or wok, sauté onion, garlic cloves, flour or arrowroot, ginger, shaved orange skin, several leaves of mint in peanut oil, plus coriander and cilantro. Cook down and set aside to drain in colander. Into 1 quart boiling water, add chopped broccoli florets, shrimp and soba noodles. Cook until tender, and add previously cooked and sautéed ingredients. Yield: 4 servings.

Rice noodles can be substituted.   *Franc Palaia*

Etsuko's Fabulous Soup

3 c. fat-free, low-sodium
  chicken broth
1 c. bottled clam juice
1 T. fish sauce
2 tsp. minced garlic
1 1/2 tsp. minced ginger
3/4 tsp. red curry paste
1 (8 oz.) pkg. sliced mushrooms
1 (3 oz.) pkg. trimmed snow peas

1/2 lb. peeled & deveined lg. shrimp
1/2 lb. skinless, boneless chicken
  breast, cut into 1" pieces
1/4 c. fresh lime juice
2 T. sugar
2 T. chopped fresh cilantro
2 T. (1/2") sliced green onion tops
1 (13.5 oz.) can light coconut milk

Combine chicken broth, clam juice, fish sauce, garlic, ginger and curry paste in a large Dutch oven, stirring with a whisk. Add mushrooms; bring to a boil. Reduce heat; simmer 4 minutes. Add snow peas, shrimp and chicken; bring to a boil. Cover, reduce heat and simmer 3 minutes. Stir in lime juice and remaining ingredients. Cook 2 minutes, or until thoroughly heated. Yield: 4 servings.

This soup has a wonderful fresh flavor. *Etsuko Bjork*

♥ Grandma's Chicken Soup

3 chicken quarters
3 lb. carrots

1 1/2 bunches celery, including leaves
Salt & pepper, to taste

Use an 8-quart pot. Wash chicken quarters. Cut off excess fat and remove skin (optional); salt and pepper pieces. Put chicken in pot; fill pot 3/4-full of water, bring to a boil, then lower heat so soup is barely boiling for 10 to 15 minutes. Skim off fat that rises to surface. Peel and chop the carrots into bite-size pieces and add to pot. Clean and chop celery and add. Now, fill pot to the top with water, and bring to a low boil, partially cover with lid. Cook for 2 hours, stirring occasionally and adding more water if necessary to keep pot full.

This tastes even better the next day! Refrigerate and skim off fat before reheating. *Jack Schachner*

Tabbuleh

1 c. bulgar	1 carrot, shredded
2 c. water	1/2 c. sweet red pepper
1/4 c. red onion	1 cucumber
1/4 c. lemon or lime juice	1/4 c. flat leaf parsley
1 can chick peas	Salt & pepper
2 lg. juicy tomatoes	Olive oil & Cheddar cheese (opt.)

Boil water; add bulgar. Cover and simmer on lowest heat for 5 minutes. Turn off heat and let stand for another 10 minutes, covered. Meanwhile, finely chop onion and parsley, and squeeze lemon or lime. Cut all vegetables into bite-size chunks. Put bulgar in a large bowl and add all the vegetables and lemon. Let stand for 1/2 hour in refrigerator or at room temperature. Add salt and pepper to taste, and if you'd like, about 1/4 cup of oil and a handful of cheese cut into bite-size cubes. Can be served on a bed of lettuce.

Ethel

"You can put everything, and the more things the better, into a salad, as into a conversation; but everything depends upon the skill of mixing."
Charles Dudley Warner (1871)

Jessie Loft's Couscous Salad

3 T. butter	1/3 c. pine nuts, toasted in heavy
1 1/2 c. vegetable stock	frying pan
1 1/2 c. couscous	1/4 c. chopped parsley
1 1/2 c. diced celery	1/4 c. lemon juice
2/3 c. currants	1/2 c. olive oil
Craisins, to taste	1/4 tsp. cinnamon
1/3 c. scallions, sliced	

Boil stock; turn off heat. Add couscous. Cover pan. Add butter and let stand 4 minutes. Remove couscous to large bowl and fluff with fork; let cool. Make dressing of olive oil, lemon juice and cinnamon; add to couscous and toss. Add celery, currants, Craisins, scallions, pine nuts and parsley; toss to mix. Let stand at room temperature at least 1 hour.

Jessie Loft

Mediterranean Salad

1 bunch romaine or curly lettuce
1 handful mesclun
1 handful arugula
Several green, red or black
   pitted olives
2 T. extra-virgin olive oil
2 T. cider vinegar
Dash of ground oregano
Dash of ground parsley

Salt & pepper, to taste
Several walnuts
1/2 avocado
1/2 red or yellow apple
1 tsp. sesame seeds
Dash of balsamic vinegar
Several grape tomatoes
1 T. raisins
Dash of ground basil

Clean and cut the lettuce into medium-size pieces. Combine with olives, grape tomatoes, a handful of mesclun, arugula, walnuts, avocado (cut in small pieces), sesame seeds, raisins, cubed apple, olive oil, apple cider vinegar, balsamic vinegar, oregano, parsley, basil, salt and pepper; mix together and eat. Yield: 4 servings.

Always try to use organic ingredients.   *Franc Palaia*

Potato-Egg Salad

4 eggs, hard-boiled
3 sm. potatoes
2 T. cottage cheese
2 to 4 T. mayonnaise
1/2 tsp. onion powder

1/4 tsp. salt
1/8 tsp. white pepper
Paprika or scallions or chives
Lettuce & cherry tomatoes

Cut potatoes into bite-sized pieces and boil until ready, but firm (6 to 8 minutes). Drain and rinse with cold water. Slice eggs with egg slicer lengthwise and again widthwise, or finely chop. Combine all ingredients in medium-sized bowl. Start with 2 tablespoons mayonnaise and add more to taste. Garnish with paprika or scallions or chives. Serve on a bed of lettuce, surrounded by tomatoes. Yield: 3 to 4 servings.

Variations: For a heart-healthy version, use the whites of 7 eggs and 1 yolk, instead of 4 eggs.

For a different taste altogether, omit above spices and add 1 teaspoon curry powder (more to taste), 1/2 teaspoon cumin and 1/4 teaspoon salt. Garnish with scallions or chives.

Tip: To hard-boil eggs. Place gently in saucepan, add water. When water boils, turn off heat. Cover tightly with lid and leave on stove-top for 15 minutes. This method helps prevent breakage. Lightly smash and roll the hard-boil egg on a counter, and peel under cold water.

Gertrude

Warm Goat Cheese Salad

1 c. Japanese bread crumbs
(Planko-Adams or Asian section),
or 1 c. bread crumbs (not soft)
1 T. chopped fresh parsley
1 T. chopped fresh basil
1 T. chopped fresh thyme
1/2 tsp. freshly-ground pepper
1/4 tsp. salt

2 (8 oz.) logs fresh goat cheese,
cut in 1" thick pieces
2 lg. egg whites, hand-beaten
until foamy
1 T. olive oil
6 to 8 slices grilled crusty bread
(olive bread is especially good)
2 pkg. spring mix salad greens

VINAIGRETTE:
2 garlic cloves, peeled & halved
1/4 c. extra-virgin olive oil

1 T. chopped fresh basil
1 1/2 to 2 T. red wine vinegar
1 1/2 to 2 T. Dijon mustard

Salad: Mix Planko, parsley, basil, thyme, pepper and salt in medium bowl to blend. Dip each cheese round in the egg whites, turning once to coat. Coat each with bread crumb mixture. Place coated rounds on plate; cover with plastic wrap and refrigerate at least 1 hour and up to 8 hours.

Heat 1 tablespoon olive oil in heavy, large nonstick skillet over medium-high heat. Add cheese rounds and cook until golden and crisp, about 3 minutes per side. Transfer to plate.

Vinaigrette: Place garlic halves and oil in small glass cup or dish. Cover tightly with plastic wrap and microwave for 30 seconds (no microwave – leave garlic halves in oil for a few hours). Transfer garlic to small bowl. Reserve oil. Using a fork, coarsely mash garlic (pieces will not break up entirely). Add basil, vinegar and mustard to garlic. Whisk until smooth. Gradually whisk in reserved garlic oil. Season with salt and pepper. (Cover and refrigerate. Let stand 1 hour at room temperature and rewhisk before using. May be made 1 day ahead.)

Place greens in large bowl and toss with all but 2 tablespoons vinaigrette, taste for seasoning. Plate the salad with 2 rounds per serving. Top rounds with remaining vinaigrette. Add pieces of grilled bread and serve. Yield: 6 to 8 servings.

Note: Fresh herbs make a difference!

Carol McGinnis

Coleslaw

1/2 head cabbage, shredded fine	1/2 tsp. salt
2 lemons or equivalent juice	1 T. sugar
2 to 3 T. mayonnaise (Hellmann's)	1 lg. carrot, grated

Mix together. Refrigerate for at least 1 hour (overnight is okay).

Enid Watsky

Cauliflower and Avocado Salad

1 med. to sm. head cauliflower	1 med. red bell pepper, cut into
1 lg. firm ripe avocado, diced	narrow, 2" strips
Juice of 1/2 lemon	2 scallions, thinly sliced

DRESSING:

2 T. olive oil	1/2 tsp. ground cumin
3 T. red wine vinegar	1/4 tsp. salt
1 tsp. dried oregano	Freshly-ground black pepper

Tomato wedges, for garnish

Break the cauliflower into bite-sized pieces and florets. Steam until tender-crisp and refresh immediately under cold water to stop the steaming. Allow the cauliflower to drain for a few minutes in a colander.

In a serving bowl, combine the diced avocado and lemon juice; toss gently. Add the cauliflower, red pepper strips and scallions.

Combine the dressing ingredients in a small bowl and stir together until well blended. Pour over the cauliflower and avocado mixture and toss gently. Cover and refrigerate for about an hour before serving. Stir once or twice during that time to distribute the dressing. Yield: 4 to 6 servings.

Adapted from "Great American Vegetarian" by **Nava Atlas**.

Mary's Endive Salad

4 bunches endive, cut in circles
1 (14 oz.) can mandarin oranges

1/4 to 1/2 lb. Swiss cheese, cut into
  strips

DRESSING:
2 T. vinegar
1/2 c. olive oil
1/2 c. salad oil

2 T. lemon juice
1/2 tsp. salt
1/4 tsp. dry mustard
1/4 tsp. paprika

Toss together endive, mandarin oranges and Swiss cheese.

Mix together olive oil and salad oil, then add vinegar, lemon juice, salt, dry mustard and paprika; toss with endive, mandarin oranges and Swiss cheese. **L. Clarke**

Broccoli Salad

2 bunches broccoli florets
1 sm. red onion
3/4 c. raisins

3/4 c. sunflower seeds
1/2 lb. cooked crisp (or crumbled)
  bacon (opt.)

DRESSING (Make the night before):
1 1/2 c. mayonnaise
1/2 c. sugar

2 T. red wine vinegar

Cut broccoli into bite-size pieces (raw). Chop or dice onion. Mix the 2 ingredients with raisins, sunflower seeds and bacon. Add the dressing. Serve cold. Yield: 10 servings. **Jayne Peckham**

Sweet Tasting Salad

1 basket fresh washed strawberries **1/2 red onion**
1 to 2 bunches washed romaine
  lettuce

DRESSING:

1/2 c. mayonnaise   **1/3 c. sugar**
1/4 c. milk   **2 T. white vinegar**

2 T. poppy seeds

Place chopped strawberries, lettuce and red onion in a bowl. Mix together mayonnaise, milk, sugar and vinegar; add dressing to salad. Sprinkle with poppy seeds.
    Enjoy!

Lori Decker

♥ African Warm Fruit Salad

2 oranges, peeled & sliced
1 grapefruit, peeled & sliced
1 doz. strawberries, cut in half
1 banana, sliced
1 (14 oz.) can pineapple slices
Powdered sugar

Vanilla (opt.) (just a few drops)
A few drops rum (opt.)
2 tsp. butter
1 stick cinnamon
1 tsp. vanilla

In a large iron skillet, melt 2 pats butter and add a stick of cinnamon and vanilla. When the butter melts, add orange slices, grapefruit slices and add the strawberries and pineapple. Add the banana last. When the fruits start cooking and blending together, shake the pan to even out the liquids. Serve warm with powdered sugar and rum. Yield: 4 servings.

This is a recipe invented to save fruit just before it rots in African places since there is no refrigeration.

J. C. Suares

♥ Apple Salad

1 1/4 c. Stoneyfield Farm vanilla
yogurt
1 (20 oz.) can chunk pineapple, in
its own juice
5 to 6 lg. York apples (or other
crisp apple, like Macintosh)

4 to 5 stalks celery
2 Satsuma tangerines or navel
oranges
1/4 c. raisins
1/4 c. craisins (dried cranberries)
1/4 c. chopped walnuts

In a large bowl, mix yogurt and entire can of pineapple, including juice.

Cut each apple in quarters, core and cut each quarter in half lengthwise (or in thirds for really large apples) and then into 4 or 5 pieces, widthwise. After cutting each apple, stir well into yogurt mixture so apples do not turn color. Chop celery. Peel tangerines or oranges, cut into halves or thirds and section, checking for seeds. Stir into salad. Add raisins, craisins and chopped walnuts.

You'll have a beautiful, delicious jewel of a salad. Enjoy!

Tahma Metz

♥ Pasta Salad with Chickpeas, Artichoke Hearts and Olives

8 oz. fusilli, rotini, or other short
pasta shape
1 c. canned chickpeas, drained &
rinsed
1 (6 oz.) jar marinated artichoke
hearts, chopped, with liquid
1/2 c. chopped & pitted black olives,
preferably cured

1 med. red bell pepper, cut into
short, narrow strips
1 lg. carrot, peeled & thinly sliced
1/4 c. finely-chopped fresh parsley
1 T. extra-virgin olive oil, or more to
taste
2 T. white balsamic or white wine
vinegar, or more to taste
Salt & freshly-ground black pepper

Cook the pasta in plenty of rapidly-simmering water until al dente. Drain and rinse under cool water, then drain well again.

Meanwhile, combine the chickpeas, artichoke hearts and liquid, olives, red pepper, carrot and parsley in a large serving bowl. Add the pasta and toss together. Add the oil and vinegar, then season to taste with salt and pepper; toss again. Cover and refrigerate until needed, or serve at once. Yield: 4 to 6 servings.

Adapted from "Pasta East to West" by **Nava Atlas**.

The ingredients given for this delectable salad can be easily doubled to make it party-sized.

Chicken Curry Salad

1/2 c. mayonnaise
1/4 c. plain yogurt
2 T. curry powder
2 c. cooked, cubed chicken
1/2 c. sliced celery
2 T. chopped scallions
1/2 c. shredded carrots

1/2 c. golden raisins
1/2 c. fresh mango, cubed (or
   apple or pear)
2 cloves garlic, minced
1/4 c. slivered almonds
1 c. broccoli florets (opt.)

Combine mayonnaise, yogurt and curry powder in a small bowl; set aside. Combine remaining ingredients in a large bowl; mix well. Fold in the dressing. Chill for at least 1 hour. Yield: 4 servings.

Virginia Donovan

Lobster Salad

2 T. fresh lemon or lime juice
1/2 c. mayonnaise
12 oz. cooked lobster, cut into 1/2"
    pieces
1/4 c. diced cucumber

1/4 c. chopped onion
1/4 c. chopped celery
1/4 c. chopped green pepper
Salt & pepper, to taste
Dash of hot pepper sauce

Combine lemon or lime juice and mayonnaise. Gently toss with lobster, cucumber, onion, celery, green pepper, salt, pepper and hot sauce.

Garnish with lemon slices, if desired.
Sandy Miller

Chili
and Stews

Seth Nadel
Red Onions with Knife
Oil on Canvas

One thing I am proud of during my tenure as director of the Barrett House was the establishment of the Chili Dinner each December after the Members' Holiday Exhibition. In those day, two huge pots of chili would simmer on the stove in the office kitchen waiting to be served to the hoards of hungry artists in the evening. Following is the original recipe which has been modified for the "at home" cook:

Wayne Lempka

Tom Barrett
Potbelly Stove
Woodcut

Chili and Stews

The Original Barrett House Chili

4 T. vegetable oil
2 onions, chopped
6 cloves garlic, minced
3 lb. lean ground chuck
1 1/2 tsp. salt
6 T. Hungarian hot chili powder

1 (28 oz.) can unpeeled,
   crushed tomatoes
1 (6 oz.) can tomato paste
Water, as necessary during
   cooking

Heat the oil in a deep pan. Stir in onions and garlic; cook until they are soft. Add the beef and salt; cook until the meat loses its pink color. Add the chili powder, crushed tomatoes and tomato paste. Taste to correct seasonings and simmer for about 1 hour, checking the liquid level and adding water when need be. Yield: 6 servings.

Serve in bowls with grated Cheddar Cheese and sour cream toppings. Have a glass of good red wine on the side to toast Betty and Tom Barrett!

Wayne Lempka

Jeep's Black Bean Brazilian Chili

2 lb. stew meat or steak
1 lb. kielbasa
2 onions
4 bay leaves
4 cloves garlic

2 T. butter
4 lg. cans black beans
4 oz. beer
Salt & pepper, to taste
Sour cream

Start 3 days ahead of time. Cut beef and kielbasa into bite-size pieces. Chop onions. Brown onions and garlic in butter. Add beef and kielbasa and brown. Pour in beer. Stir. Drain 2 cans of beans and add to mixture. Then add 2 cans beans with liquid to the pot. Add bay leaves. Stir it all up and bring to a boil. Lower heat and simmer 2 hours or so. Put it in the refrigerator when cool. Then next night, bring to a boil again and simmer for a couple more hours. Cool and put back into the refrigerator. The third night, heat and serve with sour cream. Salt and pepper to taste along the way.

Jeep Johnson

Ginger's Chili

2 lb. ground beef
2 T. olive oil
2 lg. onions, chopped
6 cloves garlic, chopped
3 T. chili powder
1 tsp. salt
1 T. paprika

1 tsp. oregano
4 T. ground cumin
1/2 tsp. cayenne pepper
1/2 c. beef stock
1 (28 oz.) can tomatoes
3 (1 lb.) cans red kidney beans
1 tsp. hot sauce of choice

Heat olive oil in large skillet and brown beef, discarding as much of the fat as possible. Add onions and garlic; cook about 3 minutes. Transfer to large, heavy pot. Add chili powder, salt, paprika, oregano, cumin, cayenne pepper, beef stock, tomatoes and kidney beans. Bring to a boil; lower heat and simmer for at least 1 hour. Add hot sauce near end of cooking time.

Serving Hints: Pass sour cream, grated Cheddar cheese, sliced onions that have been rinsed in cold water.

Ginger Nihal

Chili

1 lg. onion, sliced
2 c. celery, diced
2 c. mushrooms, sliced
2 T. canola oil
1 lb. ground turkey or beef
2 (28 oz.) cans stewed
   tomatoes

2 (16 oz.) cans & 1 (12 oz.)
   can red &/or white beans,
   rinsed
3 T. chili powder
Carrots, cut in 1" chunks
2 T. lemon juice
2 T. soy sauce
Garlic, crushed, minced or
   powder

Sauté the onion, celery and mushrooms in canola oil. Combine the turkey, tomatoes, beans, carrots, chili powder, lemon juice, soy sauce and garlic (to taste) in a large pot. Add the sautéed ingredients and slow cook for about 2 hours.

Enid Watsky

♥ Graham Kerr's Texas Chili

1 1/2 tsp. non-aromatic olive oil, divided
8 oz. bottom round, cut in fine dice
8 oz. turkey thigh, cut in fine dice
1 onion, cut into 1/4" dice
1 (10 3/4 oz.) can tomato purée
2 jalapeño peppers, seeded & chopped (leave the seeds if you like it hot)
1 (4 oz.) can diced green chilies
1 tsp. ground cumin

1 tsp. dried oregano
1/4 tsp. cayenne pepper
1 T. cocoa
1/4 tsp. salt
1 1/2 c. dealcoholized red wine or beef stock
1 1/2 c. low-sodium beef stock or water
3 cloves garlic, bashed & chopped
1 T. cornmeal
1 1/2 c. cooked brown rice
3 c. canned pinto beans, rinsed & drained

GARNISH:
1/2 c. finely-chopped raw onions

1/2 c. chopped cilantro
6 T. Parmesan cheese

Mix 1 teaspoon of the oil with the diced beef. Drop into a hot pan to brown. When it's pretty well browned, about 2 minutes, add the turkey and continue cooking 2 more minutes. Tip out onto a plate.

Heat the remaining oil in the unwashed pan and sauté the onion until it starts to wilt, 2 to 3 minutes. Add the jalapeños, diced chilies, cumin, oregano, cayenne pepper, cocoa and salt. Cook 1 minute longer. Pour in the wine and stock, bring to a boil, reduce the heat and simmer 30 minutes. Stir in the garlic and cornmeal. Cook 3 or 4 minutes, until the chili thickens. Divide the rice and beans among 6 hot bowls. Ladle the chili over the top and pass the garnishes at the table.

Ann Nihal

Turkey Chili

2 lb. ground turkey
4 cans beans (2 Progresso dark red, 2 Progresso red kidney)

1 med. can tomato sauce
2 cans Del Monte zesty chunky tomatoes, chili style
1 T. chili powder

In a large stew pot, brown turkey and then throw in all ingredients. Cook until heated through.

Serve over rice and top with Cheddar cheese if you like.

Andrea Hanson

♥ Turkey Chili
(Medium-Hot)

1 lg. onion, diced
2 garlic cloves, minced or
   thinly sliced
2 red chilies, chopped, with
   seeds discarded
1 1/4 lb. ground turkey or
   chicken

1 (14 1/2 oz.) can crushed
   tomatoes, preferably fire-
   roasted (available at health
   food store)
1 (14 1/2 oz.) can black beans
1/8 tsp. cumin
1/8 tsp. cinnamon
Salt, to taste

Sauté onion in large skillet or Dutch oven, stirring frequently, until translucent. Add garlic and jalapeños close to end of onion cooking time. Add meat to vegetables and continue to sauté, crumbling and stirring meat so all parts get browned. Continue until all pink or red is gone from meat. Add beans, tomatoes, cumin, cinnamon and salt. Stir thoroughly and heat thoroughly. Yield: 4 to 6 servings.
Preparation time: 40 to 60 minutes.

Connye Eby

♥ Black Bean Chili

1 T. olive oil
1 onion, chopped
2 sweet red peppers, chopped
1 jalapeño pepper
10 mushrooms, quartered
6 fresh plum tomatoes, cut in
   eighths
1 c. corn kernels
1 tsp. black pepper

1 tsp. ground cumin
1 T. chili powder
4 c. canned black beans, rinsed
   (12 to 13 oz. cans)
1 1/2 c. vegetable broth
1 tsp. salt
1 lb. fresh spinach, cleaned &
   chopped

Heat oil in saucepan. Add onion, red pepper, jalapeño, mushrooms, tomatoes, corn, black pepper, cumin and chili powder. Cook over medium-high heat for 10 minutes. Add beans, broth and salt. Cook for 10 minutes. Add spinach and cook until it is wilted. Serve with rice. Yield: 2 to 4 servings.

Leslie Waxtel

There are over 200 varieties of chili pepper. Though they are known for their heat, many are quite mild and rich-flavored.

♥ A "Meaty" Vegetarian Chili

1 lg. onion
1 stalk celery
2 carrots
2 peppers (I suggest 1 yellow
  & 1 red)
1 jalapeño pepper
1 (12 oz.) pkg. Lightlife Smart
  ground (this is a meat
  replacement soy product)
1 (28 oz.) can Rienzi crushed
  tomatoes, peeled (or any
  brand whole tomatoes,
  chopped)
1 (19 oz.) can red kidney beans
1 c. string beans, chopped
2 T. chili powder (or to taste)
2 tsp. ground cumin
2 T. fresh basil, chopped
Grated cheese

Chop onion. Put 1/2-inch of water in 5-quart pot or use a little oil to sauté onion. While that is cooking, chop and add celery, carrots, pepper, the Smart ground, tomatoes, kidney beans, string beans and spices. Cover and cook until vegetables are tender, about 20 to 30 minutes. Stir occasionally. Serve with grated cheese. Yield: 3 to 4 servings, depending on your appetite!

Lightlife Smart ground is a soybean based meat alternative which you can find in the refrigerator section of most health food stores.

Cassie Chu

♥ Mild Vegetable Chili

1 T. olive oil
1 sweet red or green pepper,
  chopped
1 sm. zucchini, chopped
2 cloves garlic, minced
1 (16 oz.) can chopped
  tomatoes
1 (12 to 13 oz.) can red kidney
  beans
1 (12 to 13 oz.) can white
  kidney beans or black
  beans or pinto beans
1 (4 oz.) can mild chopped green
  chilies
1 T. ground cumin
1 T. ground chili
Rice, prepared according to
  pkg. directions
1 sm. onion, chopped
Chopped parsley (opt.)
Hot sauce (opt.)

Sauté zucchini, sweet pepper and garlic in olive oil in saucepan for 2 to 3 minutes at medium heat. Vegetables will be crisp. Add beans, tomatoes and chilies. Stir in cumin and chili. Simmer at low heat for 20 minutes, stirring occasionally. Spoon into bowls over rice. Sprinkle with chopped onion and parsley and hot sauce as desired. Serve with warm tortillas or corn chips. Yield: 4 to 6 servings.

Leslie Waxtel

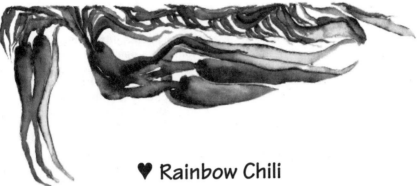

♥ Rainbow Chili

1 c. barley
2 1/2 c. water
2 c. crushed tomato
1 lg. onion, chopped
2 cloves garlic, chopped
1 stalk celery
1 to 2 carrots
1/2 lb. mushrooms
1 red pepper

1 yellow pepper
1 jalapeño pepper
1 can red kidney beans
1/2 c. edamame shelled
   soybeans
1/2 lb. fresh spinach
2 T. chili powder
2 tsp. cumin
Salt & pepper, to taste

Bring water and tomatoes to a boil. Add barley, onion and garlic. Let boil, cover and put on low heat to simmer. Stir occasionally and add more water if barley absorbs all this and is still firm. Cook 1 hour. While this is cooking, chop up the rest of the vegetables to bite-size pieces. Add them after barley has cooked for 1/2 hour, along with the spices. If you would prefer, you can bake this in the oven at 350° in a covered dish. This solves the problem of the barley sticking to the bottom of the pot. Either way, stir occasionally. Serve with salad and fresh bread. Top with grated cheese. Yield: 4 to 6 servings.

Edamame shelled soybeans can be found in the freezer section of most health food stores. They are a good source of protein.

This recipe is very flexible. Omit whatever vegetables you don't care for and add whatever you like! Some suggestions: sweet potatoes, another can of beans, green peppers, more hot peppers or summer squash.

Claudia Gorman

♥ Tofu Chili

1 lg. onion, chopped
2 carrots
2 stalks celery
2 bell peppers of your choice
(I use 1 red, 1 yellow)
1 to 2 jalapeño peppers
1 zucchini or yellow squash
1/4 lb. spinach or kale (opt.)
1 c. cooked (preferably whole
wheat) pasta, any bite-size
shape
1 lb. tofu, extra-firm

1 (28 oz.) can Rienzi crushed
tomatoes, peeled, or any can
whole tomatoes, chopped up
2 (14 to 19 oz.) cans beans of
your choice (try kidney &
cannellini)
2 T. chili powder
2 tsp. cumin
Salt & pepper, to taste
1/4 c. fresh parsley
Grated Cheddar or Romano
cheese

This recipe will fill a 5-quart pot. Sauté onion in a little oil, water or wine (your choice). Chop and add the following vegetables, in this order, and stir after each addition: celery, carrots, bell peppers, jalapeño peppers and kale. Add canned tomatoes, beans, tofu, chili powder and cumin. Stir, cover and simmer for 10 minutes. Add zucchini or yellow squash (and spinach). Stir, cover, and simmer for 10 minutes. Add cooked pasta, salt and pepper (to taste) and parsley. Cover and simmer 5 minutes. Vegetables should be soft but not mushy. Serve with grated cheese. Yield: 4 to 6 servings.

Dinner will be ready in less than one hour.

Other vegetables that work well with this chili: eggplant (put in with tomatoes and beans) or precooked winter squash or sweet potatoes (put in with pasta). Serve with fresh whole wheat bread and/or salad.

Anne Schachner

♥ Vegetarian Chili

1 lg. onion
1 clove garlic
1 T. oil
4 c. mushrooms, sliced
2 c. celery, sliced
1 1/2 c. carrots, sliced

2 (15 oz.) cans kidney beans
1 (16 oz.) can tomatoes
1 (15 oz.) can tomato sauce
3 T. dried chilies
2 T. chili powder
1 tsp. cumin

Sauté onions and garlic in oil until soft. Stir in mushrooms, celery and carrots; sauté 1 minute. Add all other ingredients. Cook, covered, on low heat for 45 minutes. Uncovered 10 minutes more.

Vera Munson

Ann's Stew

3 lg. onions, sliced
1 1/2 lb. stewing beef
2 T. mustard
1 btl. (or can) beer or ale
1 (8 oz.) can tomato sauce
2 to 3 T. red wine vinegar
3 T. brown sugar
Salt & pepper, to taste

5 cloves garlic, sliced
2 tsp. thyme
4 bay leaves
1 (28 oz.) can tomatoes with
   juice
Hot sauce, to taste
4 carrots, sliced into rounds
2 cubes beef bouillon

Sauté onions and garlic in large skillet 15 minutes or so. Add stewing beef; cook about 10 minutes more. Add thyme, mustard, bay leaves, salt and pepper. Cook 10 minutes on medium heat. Add beer, can of tomatoes, tomato sauce, hot sauce, red wine vinegar, carrots, brown sugar and bouillon. Cook an hour or so on medium-high heat (simmer). Serve with French bread.

Ann Burgener

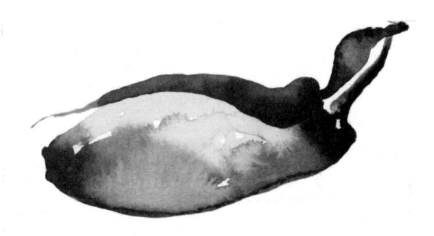

Karl's Beer Stew

1 lb. lean beef stew
1 potato, chopped in small
  pieces
1 onion, finely chopped
3 carrots, chopped in small
  pieces
1 parsnip, chopped in small
  pieces
Selection of soup greens
1 stalk celery, chopped in
  small pieces

1 to 2 cloves garlic
1 can beer
1 Jerusalem artichoke (sunchoke),
  if in season, chopped
  in small pieces
2 to 3 T. flour
Salt & pepper
Hot pepper, to taste
Cooking oil

For this stew you will need a large (9-inch or more) iron frying pan and a lidded kettle or Dutch oven. Cut the meat into bite-size pieces. In a bowl, mix flour, salt and pepper. Dredge the meat in this mixture. Heat oil in frying pan. Sear meat on all sides. Once done, put in stew pot. Put onion and garlic in frying pan. Add the other vegetables. Sauté lightly and add to stew pot. Put stew pot on medium heat. Add beer. If ingredients are submerged, add water to cover them. Cover and cook until vegetables and meat are cooked through but not overdone, about 1 hour. Stir occasionally.

Leftovers can be stored in small plastic containers in the freezer. Good for the single person to use over several weeks.

Karl Volk

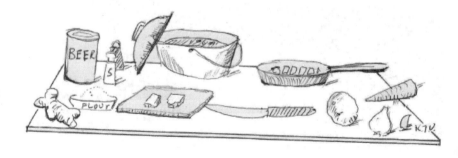

♥ Curried Vegetable Stew

Spicy and savory, this hearty curry becomes the centerpiece of a satisfying meal served over hot cooked grains and accompanied by Chapatis and a simple, palate-cooling salad of sliced cucumbers in yogurt.

2 T. canola oil
1 med. onion, chopped
2 to 3 cloves garlic, minced
2 c. baby carrots
1 med. eggplant, peeled & diced
2 med. potatoes, scrubbed & diced
1 lg. green or red bell pepper, diced
1 (16 oz.) can stewed or diced tomatoes, undrained
1 tsp. grated fresh ginger

1 to 2 fresh chilies, seeded & minced, or canned, chopped green chilies (mild or hot), to taste
1 to 2 tsp. good-quality curry powder, to taste
1 c. frozen green peas, thawed
1/4 c. chopped fresh cilantro (opt.)
Salt, to taste
Hot cooked grains (basmati rice, barley or couscous) (opt.)

Heat the oil in a soup pot and add the onion, garlic and baby carrots. Sauté over medium heat until the onion is golden, stirring frequently, about 10 minutes. Add the eggplant, potatoes, bell pepper, tomatoes, ginger, chilies and curry powder or garam marsala and 2 cups water. Bring to a simmer, then cook, covered, at a gentle simmer until the vegetable are tender but not overdone.

Stir in the peas and cilantro and season to taste with salt. Taste for spiciness and adjust the seasonings as desired. Mash some of the potato dice with a wooden spoon to thicken the cooking liquid. Simmer over low heat, covered, for an additional 5 to 10 minutes. The vegetables should be enveloped in a thick liquid. Add a small amount of additional water, if necessary. Serve in bowls, alone or over hot cooked grains. Yield: 6 to 8 servings.

Variations: You may substitute other vegetables for the ones listed above. Instead of eggplant, try substituting a medium head of cauliflower, chopped into bite-sized pieces, or use corn kernels in place of the peas. Sweet potato may be used in place of white potato.

Adapted from "Vegetarian Soups for All Seasons" by **Nava Atlas**.

"John's No Red Meat Jambalaya"

SEASONING MIX:

2 whole bay leaves
2 tsp. ground red pepper,
  preferably cayenne (makes
  it moderately spicy, adjust
  to taste)

1 1/2 tsp. salt
1 1/2 tsp. white pepper
1 tsp. dried thyme leaves
1/2 tsp. black pepper
1/4 tsp. rubbed sage

VEGETABLE MIX:

1 c. chopped onion
1 c. chopped celery

1/2 c. chopped red bell pepper
1/2 c. chopped green bell pepper
2 T. unsalted butter

1/4 lb. chopped smoked turkey,
  about 1 c. (use turkey parts
  that have been smoked, NOT
  turkey from the deli)

1/4 lb. turkey kielbasa, about 1 c.*

*Be careful to find one that has no beef or pork added. If you can't find it, just double the amount of smoked turkey.

3/4 lb. boneless chicken,
  cut into bite-sized pieces,
  about 2 c.

1 T. minced garlic
1 (No. 28) can plum tomatoes,
  chopped, with juice

4 c. chicken stock (canned is
  ok, low-sodium if you can)
2 c. uncooked rice

Combine seasoning mix in a small bowl and set aside. Chop and combine vegetable mix. Melt the butter in a large saucepan over high heat. Add the smoked turkey and cook until the meat starts to brown, about 3 minutes, stirring frequently. Add the kielbasa and cook until the meat starts to brown, about 3 minutes, stirring frequently. Add the chicken and continue cooking until the chicken is brown, about 5 minutes, stirring frequently and scraping the pan bottom well. Stir in the seasoning mix, the garlic, and half of the vegetable mixture. Cook until the vegetables start to get tender, about 5 to 8 minutes, stirring frequently and scraping the pan bottom as needed. Stir in the tomatoes and their juice and cook for 1 minute. Stir in the remaining vegetable mix. Stir in the stock and rice, mixing well. Lower heat, cover and cook until rice is tender and liquid is absorbed. If you need a little more liquid, add some stock or water. If there is too much liquid, remove the cover for the last few minutes of cooking. Yield: 6 generous servings. **_John Pagliarulo_**

Entrées

Ann Nihal
Untitled
Watercolor on Paper

MEAT ROASTING GUIDE

Cut	Weight Pounds	Approx. Time (Hrs.) (325°)	Internal Temp.
BEEF			
Standing Rib Roast (10-inch ribs)	4	1 3/4	140° (rare)
Allow 30 min. longer for 8-inch cut		2	160° (medium)
		2 1/2	170° (well done)
	8	2 1/2	140° (rare)
		3	160° (medium)
		4 1/2	170° (well done)
Rolled Ribs	4	2	140° (rare)
		2 1/2	160° (medium)
		3	170° (well done)
	6	3	140° (rare)
		3 1/4	160° (medium)
		4	170° (well done)
Rolled Rump	5	2 1/4	140° (rare)
		3	160° (medium)
		3 1/4	170° (well done)
Sirloin Tip	3	1 1/2	140° (rare)
Roast only if high		2	160° (medium)
quality, otherwise braise		2 1/4	170° (well done)
LAMB			
Leg	6	3	175° (medium)
		3 1/2	180° (well done)
	8	4	175° (medium)
		4 1/2	180° (well done)
VEAL			
Leg (piece)	5	2 1/2 - 3	170° (well done)
Shoulder	6	3 1/2	170° (well done)
Rolled Shoulder	3-5	3 - 3 1/2	170° (well done)

POULTRY ROASTING GUIDE

Type of Poultry	Ready-To-Cook Weight	Oven Temp.	Approx. Total Roasting Time
TURKEY	6-8 lbs.	325°	2 1/2 - 3 hrs.
	8-12 lbs.	325°	3 - 3 1/2 hrs.
	12-16 lbs.	325°	3 1/2 - 4 hrs.
	16-20 lbs.	325°	4 - 4 1/2 hrs.
	20-24 lbs.	325°	5-6 hrs.
CHICKEN	2 - 2 1/2 lbs.	400°	1 - 1 1/2 hrs.
(Unstuffed)	2 1/2 - 4 lbs.	400°	1 1/2 - 2 1/2 hrs.
	4-8 lbs.	325°	3-5 hrs.
DUCK	3-5 lbs.	325°	2 1/2 - 3 hrs.
(Unstuffed)			

NOTE: Small chickens are roasted at 400° so that they brown well in the short cooking time. They may also be done at 325° but will take longer and will not be as brown. Increase cooking time 15 to 20 minutes for stuffed chicken and duck.

Entrées

♥ Barbecued Veal

2 lb. veal, cut in 1" cubes
1 med. onion, sliced
4 T. catsup
2 T. Worcestershire sauce

1/4 c. water & 1/4 c. cider vinegar, combined
1 c. water
1 tsp. paprika
2 T. sugar

Dredge veal in flour and brown with onion. Add the rest of the ingredients. Simmer for 1 1/2 hours. Serve over rice.

Joanne Rein

Veal Chops on a Bed of Mesclun Salad

4 (3/4" thick) loin veal chops, about 8 oz. each
1/2 c. seasoned bread crumbs (your favorite brand or make your own by adding dried thyme, oregano & basil to plain bread crumbs)
1/2 c. freshly-grated Parmesan cheese
4 ripe plum tomatoes, chopped & seeded

1/2 c. finely-chopped red onion
1 c. chopped arugula leaves
5 T. olive oil
Dash (or two) red wine vinegar
Salt & freshly-ground pepper, to taste
4 c. tightly-packed mesclun salad
2 to 3 T. balsamic vinaigrette (make your own or buy)

Place veal chops between 2 pieces of waxed paper and pound meat as thin as you can, up to 1/2-inch from bone. Combine Parmesan cheese and bread crumbs in a flat dish and coat chops thoroughly with mixture, pressing as much as you can onto each chop. Combine tomatoes, red onion, arugula, 2 tablespoons olive oil, red wine vinegar, salt and pepper in a bowl.

Heat remaining 3 tablespoons olive oil in a skillet and brown veal chops about 3 minutes on each side. Place mesclun in a bowl and drizzle balsamic vinaigrette over salad; toss gently. Divide mesclun onto 4 plates.

Transfer chops to plates, placing a chop on each mesclun salad portion, and top each chop with a large spoonful of tomato arugula mixture. Yield: 4 portions.

This dish makes a lovely summer supper presentation. Enjoy!

Helene Small

Purerco Pibil
(Slow-Roasted Pork)

5 T. annatto seeds
2 tsp. cumin seeds
1 T. black pepper
8 allspice balls
1/2 tsp. cloves
2 habanero peppers, chopped & seeded
1/2 c. orange juice

1/2 c. white vinegar
2 T. salt
8 cloves garlic
Juice of 5 lemons
Splash of tequila
5 lb. pork butt
12 banana leaves

Grind annatto seeds, cumin, pepper, allspice and cloves in a coffee grinder (used only for spices) until it becomes a fine powder. Put orange juice, vinegar, peppers and powder into blender and blend until smooth. Add salt, garlic, lemon juice and tequila; blend until smooth.

Cut pork butt into 2-inch cubes. Put meat into Ziploc bag with blended liquid. Mush around until the meat is covered. Line a roasting pan with banana leaves. Empty contents of Ziploc bag onto leaves and cover with more banana leaves; cover and seal the pan with tinfoil. Cook for 4 hours at 325°. Yield: 5 servings.

I found all the ingredients at Casa Latina, Main St., Poughkeepsie.

Jeff Johnson,
From Robert Rodriguez

Thai Steak Salad

12 oz. boneless steak, cooked medium-rare
Salad, made of romaine lettuce
1 med. cucumber (slices)

1 pkg. radish slices
1 bunch scallions
1 bunch cilantro

DRESSING:
1/2 c. chicken broth
2 T. lime juice
1 1/2" x 1" piece ginger, peeled & coarsely chopped

1 tsp. vegetable or olive oil
1 clove garlic, peeled
1 tsp. sugar
1 tsp. salt
1 tsp. hot sauce, or to taste

Broil or grill steak to desired doneness. Toss salad. Make dressing by mixing all ingredients in blender until smooth. Slice steak. Make salad and arrange steak on top. Pour dressing over all and serve.

Ann Nihal

"Cook, see all your sauces be sharp and poignant
in the palate that they may commend you."
Francis Beaumont – 1584–1616

Julian Long's Pot Roast

Pot roast, boneless chuck (3 to 4 lb.
  for 2 people)
1 lg. white onion, sliced
1/4 to 1/2 c. wine or bourbon or
  dry sherry

1 1/2 to 2 c. beef broth
1 sm. bag baby carrots, peeled & chopped
3 to 4 stalks celery, chopped
3 med.-sized potatoes
Seasonings

Brown onions in Dutch oven (cut into quarters to get rings to fall apart) in 2 to 3 tablespoons olive oil. Remove onions from pan; brown meat. Sear well all over.

Remove meat (this is optional – can leave the meat in pan). Deglaze pan with wine or bourbon or dry sherry. Use enough to cook away the alcohol and clean pan sides well. Add broth (or water if preferred). Return meat (if removed) to pan. Add onion, a few carrots, some of the celery and more broth if needed. Cook, covered, for about 1 1/2 hours. Add rest of carrot, celery, chopped potatoes (optional: chopped rutabagas, leeks – go in last, and parsnips); cook for last 1/2 hour.

Julian Long

Guiness-Braised Beef Brisket

2 c. water
1 c. chopped onion
1 c. chopped carrot
1 c. chopped celery
1 c. Guiness – stout
2/3 c. packed brown sugar
1/4 c. tomato paste

1/4 c. chopped fresh, or 1 T. dried dill
1 (14 1/2 oz.) can low-salt beef broth
6 black peppercorns
2 whole cloves
1 (3 lb.) cured corned beef brisket,
   trimmed

Combine all ingredients, except the brisket, in a large electric slow-cooker, stirring until well blended. Top with beef. Cover and cook on HIGH for 8 hours, or until beef is tender.

Remove beef, cut diagonally across grain into 1/4-inch slices. Discard broth mixture (delicious as sandwich on rye bread).

From "Cooking Light", March, 2003.   ***Mario and Barbara Giampe***

Mother's Meat Loaf

2 lb. ground chuck
1 lg. can tomatoes, drained
1 egg, raw
1 onion, minced
1 clove garlic, minced

3 tsp. salt
Pepper
3/4 c. oatmeal
1 1/2 c. herbes de France
5 slices bacon

Mix all ingredients in bowl. Put in loaf pan. Bake at 350° for 1 hour with 5 slices bacon on top. Ladle some juices away. Yield: 8 servings.

L. Clarke

Mishy-Mosh

1 lg. onion, sliced
2 c. celery, 1/2" slices
2 c. mushrooms, sliced
1 lb. chopped meat (beef or turkey)

Garlic, crushed, minced or powder
2 T. lemon juice
2 T. soy sauce

Sauté onion, celery and mushrooms in oil in large pan, until tender. Add forkfuls of chopped meat, turning until cooked. Season with lemon and soy at end. Add bean sprouts (optional). Serve over rice.

Enid Watsky

♥ Chicken Fruité

8 oz. chicken breast, cut into strips	1 T. coarsely-grated ginger
1 tsp. olive oil	1/4 tsp. cinnamon
1 lg. onion, thinly sliced into strips	1/8 tsp. allspice
1 lg. clove garlic, minced	1 tsp. grated orange peel
1/3 c. cut dried apricots, prunes or raisins	1 c. fresh orange juice
	Freshly-ground pepper
	1 T. sugar

Sauté chicken strips in hot oil until brown on 1 side. Turn and brown on other side, adding onion and garlic. Continue sautéing until onion becomes brown and soft. Add fruit, ginger, cinnamon, allspice, orange peel, orange juice and pepper. Continue cooking over low heat just a few minutes, until meat is cooked and mixture has thickened slightly (like duck sauce). Transfer to pot and heat up. Yield: 2 servings.

Great served over rice or noodles, even spaghetti.

I never made this dish for only two because it is a great company meal, which can be made ahead of time and refrigerated, even overnight. It also freezes well, so why not make it in abundance and store it for the future.

Carol Pepper-Cooper

Roasted Chicken over Potatoes and Onions

4 chicken breasts
8 to 10 med. to lg. potatoes
2 onions
8 cloves garlic
Rosemary

Juice of 1 lemon
1/3 c. olive oil
Salt & pepper
Bacon slices (opt.)

Peel potatoes and slice. Cut onions into "boat" shapes (quartered). Layer potato slices, onions and garlic in a 9x13-inch roasting pan; season with salt and pepper. Arrange chicken breast on top; again, season with salt and pepper. Arrange fresh rosemary; pour lemon juice and olive oil over top. I also like to put the bacon slices on top to keep the chicken from getting dried out. Bake at 325° to 350° for approximately 1 hour, making sure both the chicken and the potatoes are done. Yield: 4 servings.

Kirsten Holm Schamberg

"What I say is that, if a man really likes potatoes,
he must be a pretty decent sort of fellow."
A.A. Milne (1920)

Garlicky, Cheesy Chicken

Amounts of ingredients can be varied to taste:

3 boneless, skinless chicken
   breasts
1/2 c. yogurt
1/4 c. mayonnaise

1 T. powdered garlic
3/4 c. Italian bread crumbs
1/4 to 1/2 c. grated Romano cheese
2 T. chopped parsley

Mix mayonnaise, garlic and yogurt in large bowl. Mix crumbs, cheese and parsley in separate large bowl. Dip chicken in yogurt mix, then in crumb mix. Put in greased baking pan. Add any leftover yogurt mix to baking pan. Bake in 350° oven for 20 minutes.

Sherley LaDue

It is easy to remove the skin from a chicken. Most of the fat is in the skin. Remove the wings, then cut the bird down the breastplate and lay it out flat with the back up. Pull off the skin.

♥ Chicken-in-a-Bag

1 (2 1/2 to 3 lb.) fryer	Paprika
Salt	Garlic salt
Pepper	Celery salt
Lemon peel	16 lb. brown bag
Onion salt	

Wash and dry chicken and sprinkle with seasonings, inside and out. Put in bag and twist end of bag tightly. Place on rack in 375° oven with pan below to catch drippings that leak through bag. Do not disturb for 1 1/2 hours. Chicken will be tender and juicy with a brown, crisp skin.

Note: If using chicken pieces, cook for 55 minutes.

Cynthia Dill

Raspberry Chicken

8 half chicken breasts, boneless & skinless	1/2 c. canned chicken broth, light & fat free
5 T. canola oil	1/2 c. heavy cream
1/2 c. finely-chopped yellow onions	3 T. canned, crushed tomatoes
10 T. raspberry French wine vinegar	20 (approx.) fresh raspberries

Flatten each breast by pressing it gently with the palm of your hand. Salt and pepper to taste. Melt oil in a large skillet. Raise the heat; add breasts and cook about 3 minutes per side, or until lightly colored. Careful not to brown. Remove from skillet and reserve. Add onion to fat in pan and cook, covered, over low heat until tender, about 15 minutes. Add vinegar; raise heat and cook, uncovered, stirring occasionally, until vinegar is reduced to a syrupy mixture. Whisk in chicken broth, heavy cream, crushed tomatoes and simmer 1 minute. Return breasts to skillet and simmer gently in sauce, basting until they are done and sauce has been reduced and thickened slightly, about 5 minutes.

Remove breasts with slotted spoon and arrange on serving platter. Add raspberries to sauce in skillet, swirl them in sauce by shaking the skillet. Pour sauce over breasts and serve. Yield: 8 servings.

Mildred Cohen

Easy Chicken Bake

4 chicken legs
4 chicken thighs
1 red or green pepper, cut up
Sliced mushrooms, about 1 c.

Sliced onions, about 1/2 c.
Dried basil, to taste
Wish-Bone Italian dressing (original)

Arrange onions on bottom of nonreactive baking pan. Sprinkle basil on chicken pieces. Place chicken in baking pan, along with pepper and mushrooms. Drizzle Italian dressing on chicken, mushrooms and pepper. Bake for 1 hour in 375° oven. Yield: 4 servings.

Good with rice. Or, for a complete one-dish meal, add cut-up potatoes to the other ingredients before baking.

Jean Barker

Seared Scallops and Crispy Prosciutto with Roasted Tomatoes and Mashed White Beans

6 lg. ripe plum tomatoes, quartered
Salt & freshly-ground black pepper
A pinch of dried oregano
Butter
4 to 6 slices prosciutto
3 cloves garlic, finely chopped
  or pressed
Dried red chili flakes, to taste

6 anchovy fillets, chopped, or
  anchovy paste
2 (14 oz.) cans cannelloni beans or
  flageolet beans, drained
Extra-virgin olive oil
1 lb. fresh sea scallops
Olive oil & lemon juice dressing*
1 sm. handful peppery greens
  (arugula or watercress)

*Use 2 parts lemon juice to 5 parts olive oil.

In a pan, fry the garlic, chili flakes and anchovy paste in a glug of olive oil for a minute or so. Add your beans and cook for a couple of minutes before adding a wine glass of water (1/2 cup or more if texture is too dry). Bring to a boil, then lightly mash to a coarse purée. Loosen the purée with a little more water if need be. Finish the flavor off with some peppery extra-virgin olive oil, salt and freshly-ground black pepper.

Preheat the oven to 475°. Season the tomatoes and sprinkle with oregano. Drizzle with olive oil and roast in the oven, skin-side down, for about 10 to 15 minutes. Place the prosciutto slices beside the tomatoes and continue to roast for a further 10 minutes, until the tomatoes are juicy and the prosciutto is crisp.

Season the scallops with salt and pepper, then sear them in a heavy frying pan or cast-iron griddle with a touch of butter for 2 minutes, without touching them. Check and continue to fry until they have a lovely sweet caramelized skin – turn them over and allow the other side to do the same. Don't overcook them. Remove to a bowl and coat with a little olive oil and lemon juice dressing. Put some smashed bean purée on the middle of each plate, then scatter on top the tomatoes, prosciutto and scallops. Finish off with some peppery greens. Mmmm.

Thanks to Jamie Oliver, his cookbooks are great!

Stephen Aronson

Scallops with Pecan Crust

2 lb. scallops
6 oz. roasted pecans, whole or
   pieces
4 T. flour

Parsley
Shallots (opt.)
4 T. butter or olive oil

Place pecans and flour in food processor until finely ground. Melt butter and add parsley and shallots, if desired. Put nut and flour mixture in a plastic bag and add scallops. Toss until fully-coated. Sauté in a hot pan, turning as needed, until lightly brown and just cooked through. Do not overcook, or the scallops will become rubbery.

Serve with Basmati Rice (see Side Dishes) and Carrots with Tarragon (see Side Dishes).

Laurie Bloomfield

Shrimp with Spinach and Artichoke Hearts

1 lb. frozen shrimp, cleaned &
  deveined
1 (12 oz.) bag organic spinach
6 cloves garlic
1 c. green olives

2 T. capers
1 (14 oz.) can artichoke hearts
Olive oil
1 tsp. Cajun spices
Balsamic vinegar

Season the shrimp with 1 teaspoon Cajun spices or just a little hot sauce (optional: may substitute garlic oil). Sauté in pan until almost cooked, remove from pan. Add garlic and 1/2 tablespoon oil and artichoke hearts, sautéed until golden. Add shrimp back in, capers and green olives.

In a separate pan, boil just enough water and balsamic vinegar to cover the bottom of the pan. Add spinach and cook until wilted. Drain. Serve spinach on a plate. Then spoon on the shrimp artichoke mixture. Garnish with fried tomato slices.   *Bi Bi DeFelice*

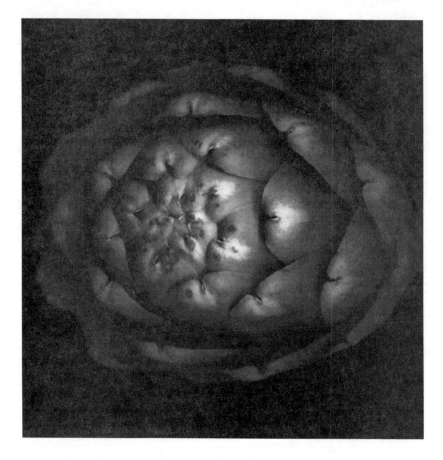

Broiled (Grilled) Salmon with Avocado and Lime Relish

4 (6 to 7 oz.) salmon fillets	1 bunch fresh chives, chopped
1 T. + 1/4 c. olive oil	1 T. fresh lime juice
1/2 lime	Salt & pepper
1 firm, ripe avocado, diced	

Rub salmon with 1 tablespoon oil. Squeeze lime over. Let stand while combining avocado, 1/4 cup oil, chives and 1 tablespoon lime juice. Season with salt and pepper.

Preheat broiler. Place salmon, skin-side down on foil-lined baking sheet. Sprinkle with salt and pepper. Broil without turning, until just opaque, approximately 10 to 15 minutes. Transfer salmon to serving plate, spoon avocado relish over and serve. Yield: 4 servings.

I have actually only used this recipe for grilling the salmon. It's delicious still. **Kirsten Holm Schamberg**

Wild Sea Bass

2 lb. wild sea bass or other firm white fish (i.e. red snapper)	4 tsp. butter
2 carrots, julienned	2 lb. fish trimmings
1 zucchini, julienned	Water
2 leeks, white part only, julienned	2 stalks lemon grass
3 T. fresh ginger, julienned	2 onions
2 stalks lemon grass, tender parts only, chopped	3 carrots
4 oz. dried shiitake mushrooms, soaked in 2 c. boiling water & then julienned	1 bunch cilantro (save 4 sprigs for garnish)
	2 T. fresh ginger
	Water, from soaking shiitake mushrooms

Divide fish into 4 portions and place each on a piece of tinfoil. Top with equal amounts of carrot, zucchini, leek, ginger, stalks lemon grass, mushrooms and butter. Close each package tightly and bake in 400° oven until fish is cooked through and flaky (approximately 15 to 20 minutes).

Meanwhile, put fish trimmings, water, 2 stalks lemon grass, onions, carrots, cilantro (minus 4 sprigs for garnish) and 2 tablespoons fresh ginger into the water from soaking the shiitake mushrooms and add enough water to fully cover all ingredients. Cook until reduced by 1/3; strain and serve with fish and rice noodles. **Laurie Bloomfield**

Sautéed Salmon with Ginger and Mushrooms

1 to 1 1/2 lb. salmon fillets
1/2 to 2/3 c. white cooking wine
1" ginger root, chopped fine or
   zested
1/4 c. lite soy sauce
3 T. margarine
1 T. oil

1 c. chicken broth or bouillon
6 to 8 mushrooms, sliced 1/4" pieces
4 to 5 scallions, green only, 3/4" slices
2 to 3 garlic cloves, chopped fine
2 tsp. cornstarch, mixed in 2 T.
   cold water

Skin salmon; cut in approximately 2-inch pieces. Sauté garlic in 3 tablespoons margarine and 1 tablespoon oil mixture. Add salmon; brown both sides. Remove and drain salmon. Pour off liquid from pan. Add wine, ginger and soy. Heat to simmer. Add back salmon; continue to cook. When 3/4 cooked, add broth/ bouillon and mushrooms. Cook until fish and mushrooms are done. Add pepper to taste. Add scallions. Thicken with cornstarch/water. Yield: 3 to 4 servings.

Serve with rice or pasta.

Carl Schwartz

Crispy Fish

1 1/2 lb. flounder fillets, sliced
   in thin strips
2 T. sherry
1/4 tsp. ground ginger
Salt & pepper
3 scallions, 1 sliced thinly
3 eggs
1 c. flour

1/2 c. cornstarch
1 c. water
6 T. ketchup
6 T. sugar
2 T. soy sauce
2 T. vinegar
1 T. sesame oil
2 T. olive oil

Mix together the salt, pepper, sherry, scallions and ginger. Add fish strips and marinate for 1 hour. Dip the fish strips in batter made of eggs, flour, cornstarch and water; deep-fry until golden brown. Remove from oil, drain; place on serving platter in warm oven until all fish is cooked.

Meanwhile, combine ketchup, sugar, soy sauce, vinegar, sesame oil and olive oil. Bring to a boil and pour over cooked fish slices. Serve with rice.

Mario and Barbara Giampe

Baked Shad

1 shad

Put heavy foil around shad. In its middle, place 3 strips of bacon and 1 lemon slice. Sprinkle with salt and pepper. Cover with 2 layers of foil. Bake in oven at 250° for 7 hours. Bones dissolve and it has a delicious flavor. Yield: 6 servings.   *L. Clarke*

♥ Steph's Swordfish

1 1/2 lb. salmon fillet or swordfish	**1/8 to 1/4 tsp. lemon pepper**
6 oz. low-sodium soy sauce	**1/8 tsp. ginger, or about 1 tsp. fresh,**
2 oz. oil	**peeled & chopped**
2 oz. red wine vinegar	**2 oz. brown sugar or honey (opt.)**
2 to 3 cloves chopped garlic, or	**Fresh lemon (opt.)**
garlic powder, to taste	

Mix all ingredients, except fish, in a jar or baggie and shake well. Pour over fish and marinate for 2 to 4 hours, turning over if marinade doesn't cover the entire fish. Grill or broil on medium heat for about 6 minutes per side, depending on thickness of fillet. Baste with marinade and squeeze fresh lemons over fish.

In a separate pot, bring the rest of the marinade to a boil, then simmer around 20 minutes and use later for reheating, or for extra marinade.

This recipe also works well with salmon.

Stephanie Brenner

Jay's Crab Cakes

1 1/2 lb. shredded crabmeat
1 1/2 lb. lump crabmeat
3 c. mayonnaise
2 eggs
1/4 c. dried parsley

1 T. Old Bay seasoning
1/4 c. yellow mustard
1/8 tsp. lemon juice
2 c. crushed saltines

Drain crabmeat and mix with crackers. In another bowl, mix together mayonnaise, eggs, parsley, seasoning, mustard and lemon juice. Mix all into crabmeat mixture. Shape into 8 crabcakes shaped like baseballs. Bake on baking sheet at 400° for 25 minutes, or until golden brown. Yield: 8 crabcakes. **Jay Nihal**

Pasta
and Noodles

Franc Palaia
Palm Tree - Sicily
Oil Crayon on 5x70 Polaroid

Pasta Guide

Macaroni:

COCHIGLIE: "Conch Shells" are shaped like seashells in varied sizes; good for salads, baking dishes and stuffing.

DITALI and **DITALINI**: "Thimbles," cut in very short lengths and good for salads.

ELBOW MACARONI: Are semi-circles made of hollow tubular pasta in many sizes, from spaghetti size to 1/2 inch around.

ELENA: A narrow rippled macaroni named after an Italian queen, and can be substituted for lasagna.

MANICOTTI: "Small muff," a tube 4 inches long and 1 inch in diameter with ends cut diagonally and is stuffed.

MOSTACCIOLI: "Small mustaches," 2-inch long hollow pasta tubes, either smooth or ridged, and used in baked dishes.

RIGATONI: Large groved hollow pasta tubes, used either with sauce or in a baking dish, substituting for mostaccioli.

Spaghetti:

FUSILLI: "Twists," spaghetti twisted in a corkscrew hairpin, also in a large spiral.

ROTE: Shaped like wheels.

LASAGNA: Latin, "lasanum" meaning "pot" a very wide spaghetti used in baked dishes.

LINGUINE: "Small tongue," a spaghetti but flatish or oval like narrow thick noodles.

Noodles:

TRENETTINE: Is a fine noodle, with **FETTUCCELLI**, then **FETTUCCINE**, and **LASAGNA** the largest.

CAVATELLI: Is a short curled noodle, similar to shell but thinner.

FARFALLE: "Butterflies" or "bowties" are usually made of eggs.

MARGHERITA: A long narrow noodle and rippled on one side.

PASTA VERDI: A green noodle, usually flavored with herbs or spinach.

RAVIOLI: Cut into squares and stuffed with cheese and meat filling. Always homemade.

TAGLIATELLE: A very wide noodle which when cooked, can be used a **TORTELLINI** dough.

TORTELLINI: "Small twists," usually homemade and stuffed.

Pasta and Noodles

Liang Mein
(Cold Noodles)

1 lb. fresh egg noodles
3 T. oil
4 T. light soy sauce
3 T. sesame paste
1 T. sesame oil
3 T. Chinese black vinegar

1 T. chili oil
2 tsp. salt
2 chopped scallions
2 cloves garlic, chopped
Chopped fresh ginger, to taste

Bring 6 cups water to boil. Add noodles. Cook 3 to 5 minutes. Drain. Add 3 tablespoons oil. Toss and chill. Mix soy sauce, sesame paste, sesame oil, Chinese vinegar, chili oil, salt, scallions, garlic and ginger together in a large bowl. Mix with cooked noodles and serve.

Diane Robbins

Mamma Mandelbaum's Lokshen Kugel

12 oz. egg noodles
1/2 c. raisins
6 eggs, separated
8 oz. cream cheese
16 oz. sour cream

2 c. milk
2/3 c. sugar (or Splenda)
1 1/2 tsp. vanilla extract
1/2 tsp. salt

Preheat oven to 350°. Lightly butter 3-quart baking dish. Beat whites to stiff peaks. Set aside.

In blender, combine yolks with cream cheese, sour cream, milk, sugar, vanilla and salt. It is convenient to blend ingredients in two batches. Transfer mixture to extra-large bowl. Fold beaten egg whites into sour cream mixture. Set aside.

Boil noodles according to package directions (usually 5 minutes). Drain noodles and toss with raisins. Mix gently with sour cream mixture. Transfer to 3-quart baking dish. Bake for 1 1/2 hours. After the first 40 minutes, loosely place aluminum sheet over Kugel to prevent burning of surface. Before serving, let Kugel rest 10 minutes, or serve next day at room temperature. Yield: 8 servings.

Maija Veide

Vegetable Lasagna

1 lb. lasagna noodles, prepared
according to pkg. directions
3 c. grated zucchini
2 (10 oz.) pkg. frozen,
chopped spinach, thawed &
drained
1 c. grated carrot
1 T. olive oil
2 cloves garlic, crushed
1/4 c. chopped fresh parsley

1 c. grated Parmesan or Romano cheese
2 1/2 c. spaghetti sauce
(homemade or jar)
1 egg
1/4 tsp. ground nutmeg
1 lb. Mozzarella cheese, sliced
thinly (whole or part-skim)
3 c. ricotta cheese (whole or
part-skim)
Salt & pepper, to taste

In mixing bowl, beat egg with ricotta, nutmeg and parsley. Mix half of ricotta mixture with the zucchini and carrots; set aside. In saucepan, sauté garlic in olive oil. Turn off heat. Add spinach and toss to mix. Add other half of ricotta mixture to spinach. Spoon 2/3 cup of the sauce into the bottom of 9x13-inch baking pan. Add a layer of noodles, then a layer of zucchini mix, then some sauce and grated cheeses. Then add another layer of noodles, then the spinach mixture, sauce, and Mozzarella cheese. Finish with a layer of noodles, sauce and cheese. Cover with aluminum foil and bake in 350° oven for 45 minutes. Uncover, bake another few minutes to brown on top. Let cool 10 minutes before cutting.

Leslie Waxtel

Spaghetti Pizza

6 oz. spaghetti (preferably
refrigerated leftover)
1 egg
2 T. milk

2 to 4 oz. shredded Mozzarella
cheese
3 heaping T. grated Romano
or Parmesan cheese
3/4 to 1 c. tomato sauce

Preheat oven to 350°. Mix cooked spaghetti with egg, milk and Romano or Parmesan cheese. Press into a lightly-oiled 9x9-inch baking dish. Spread sauce over this and sprinkle with Mozzarella cheese. Bake at 350° for 30 minutes. Cool 5 minutes before cutting. Yield: 2 to 4, depending on appetite!

Alec Schachner

Tofu Pasta Casserole

1 lb. firm tofu
1 T. olive oil
1 tsp. onion powder
2 tsp. garlic powder
1 T. parsley
1 tsp. oregano

2 tsp. basil
1 (1 qt.) jar tomato sauce
1/2 lb. pasta, shape your choice
1 c. Mozzarella or Cheddar
  cheese, grated

Drain and mash tofu. Sauté tofu, onion powder, garlic powder, parsley, oregano and basil in oil for 5 to 10 minutes. Add 1 cup tomato sauce and simmer 5 minutes. Preheat oven to 350°. Boil pasta al dente. In a 2-quart baking dish, layer 1/2 the pasta, 1 1/2 cups sauce, 1/2 tofu mixture, 1/2 the cheese; repeat layers. Bake for 30 minutes.

Anonymous

Tony Montana Pasta

1 box ziti
1 (8 oz.) goat cheese log
1 bunch Italian parsley,
  chopped
1 c. olive oil
1 (14 oz.) can black olives,
  sliced
3 lg. tomatoes, diced & seeded

1 (4 to 8 oz.) jar capers
2 tsp. salt
2 tsp. pepper
2 lg. garlic cloves, pressed
Garlic powder, to taste
Parmesan cheese
1 onion, diced

In a large saucepan, heat olive oil. Sauté garlic and onion until translucent. Add olives and capers; sauté for 1 minute. Add tomatoes and parsley. Cook until tender. Remove from heat.

Meanwhile, cook pasta according to directions on box. Drain and immediately return to pot and add goat cheese. Stir until the cheese has melted and coated all the pasta. Serve the pasta with a generous serving of the sauce on top with Parmesan cheese.

Rachel Robbins

♥ Pasta Lenticche

(Pasta with Sicilian Lentil Sauce)

3/4 c. lentils
1/2 lb. penne or ziti
2 T. extra-virgin olive oil
1 med. onion, chopped
3 to 4 cloves garlic, minced
1 med. green bell pepper, diced
1 c. sliced white or crimini
   mushrooms (opt.)

4 c. homemade marinara sauce, or
   1 (28 oz.) jar good-quality
   marinara sauce
Salt & freshly-ground black
   pepper
Grated fresh Parmesan cheese
   or Parmesan-style nondairy
   cheese, for topping (opt.)

Rinse and sort the lentils and combine them in a small saucepan with 1 1/2 cups water. Slowly bring to a simmer, then simmer very gently, covered, for 30 to 40 minutes, until they are tender but still hold their shape. Drain any excess water. Do this step ahead of time.

Cook the pasta in plenty of rapidly-simmering water until al dente, then drain.

Heat the oil in a large saucepan. Add the onion and garlic; sauté over medium-low heat until the onion is translucent. Add the bell pepper and optional mushrooms; continue to sauté until the onion is golden. Stir in the cooked lentils and marinara sauce. Slowly bring to a simmer, then simmer gently, covered, for 10 minutes. Combine the lentil sauce with the cooked pasta in a large serving container and toss together thoroughly. Season to taste with salt and pepper and serve, passing around Parmesan cheese for topping, if desired. Yield: 6 servings.

Adapted from "Pasta East to West" by **Nava Atlas**.

Cadore

Pasta with Shrimp and Vegetables for Two

3 cloves garlic, finely chopped
1 T. olive oil
3 mushrooms, or 1 small
  portobello, chopped
1 sm. zucchini, chopped into
  bite-size pieces
12 cherry tomatoes, cut in half
1 1/2 c. broccoli flowers,
  chopped bite-size

1 sm. red pepper, chopped
  bite-size
6 sun-dried tomatoes (not
  in oil), cut in quarters
12 lg. shrimp, shelled & deveined
2 c. cooked pasta (1 c. dry)
1/4 to 1/2 c. Mozzarella cheese
1/2 c. basil pesto, or make your
  own with light version*

*LIGHT VERSION OF BASIL PESTO:
3 c. fresh basil leaves
  (packed), rinsed & patted dry
2 lg. cloves garlic
1/2 c. pine nuts

1/2 c. Parmesan or Pecorino
  Romano cheese
1/4 c. olive oil
1 sm. plum tomato
Salt & pepper, to taste (opt.)

Boil water in large saucepan and cook 1 cup dry pasta (to make 2 cups cooked pasta). Drain and set aside.

If you are making the pesto, place all the pesto ingredients in a food processor until a smooth paste is formed.

If using frozen shrimp, throw in boiling water for 2 minutes to defrost. Soak sun-dried tomatoes in water. In a large skillet, sauté garlic in olive oil, 2 minutes. Add red pepper, mushrooms and broccoli. Cook, stirring, about 5 minutes. Add zucchini, cook another 3 minutes. Add drained sun-dried tomatoes and shrimp; cook 2 minutes, stirring. Add cherry tomatoes; cook 1 minute. Turn heat as low as possible and add pasta, 1/2 cup, pesto and Mozzarella cheese. Stir 1 minute to warm everything up. Serve with extra pesto, fresh bread and salad.

Cooking and preparation time: 20 to 30 minutes.

If making pesto, an additional 15 minutes.   *Marisa*

Pasta Pugliese Verde with Orecchiette

1/2 lb. macaroni, orecchiette
  or similar small-sized
  macaroni with texture
Big bunch of arugula
3 cloves garlic

1 c. olive oil
1/2 c. pine nuts or walnuts
2 T. Parmesan cheese
Salt & pepper

Clean a nice big bunch of arugula. Boil water and cook orecchiette (or substitute macaroni) while you make the pesto. Place in blender: several cloves of peeled garlic, extra-virgin olive oil, Parmesan cheese, pine nuts and arugula. Blend until creamy. Combine with cooked pasta, salt and pepper to taste. Serve hot or room temperature. Makes several servings.

This is a traditional pasta dish from Apuglia, Italy (the heel of the boot). They use Orecchiette (pasta shaped like little ears) and make a pesto out of arugula instead of basil. Any macaroni will do.

Eva D'Ambra

Fusilli with Dill Pesto

PESTO:
6 T. olive oil
4 garlic cloves, chopped
1 bunch dill

1 1/2 oz. pine nuts
1/4 c. freshly-grated Parmesan
  cheese
1 T. heavy cream

12 oz. fusilli pasta

Purée olive oil, garlic, dill, pine nuts, Parmesan cheese and cream in a blender until they make a paste. Cook pasta al dente. Drain pasta and toss with pesto. Serve immediately.

Optional: Reserve some dill for garnish.

Hint: Cilantro or parsley may be substituted for dill.

Karla Nihal

Baked Penne with Meat Sauce

8 oz. dried whole wheat penne
6 c. (approx.) Lou's Mama
  Marinara sauce or any other
  marinara sauce
1 lb. lean ground beef
1/2 c. chopped onion

1/2 c. sliced pitted black olives
  (opt.)
1/2 c. shredded reduced-fat
  Mozzarella cheese (opt.)
1/2 tsp. oregano
1/2 tsp. black pepper

Preheat oven to 375°. Cook pasta according to package directions. Drain well.

Meanwhile, in a large skillet, cook ground beef and onion until meat is brown. Drain any fat. Stir in tomato sauce; reduce heat and simmer for 10 minutes. Add olives, oregano and pepper to taste. Stir in cooked pasta. Pour mixture into large baking casserole. Bake, covered, in the preheated oven for 30 minutes. Sprinkle with Mozzarella cheese (optional). Bake, uncovered, about 5 minutes, or until cheese melts. Yield: 6 servings.

Preparation time: 15 minutes. Baking time: 30 to 40 minutes.

Freezes well.

Lisa Bacchus Aronson

Mom's Comfort Baked Macaroni and Cheese

1 (8 to 9 oz.) pkg. macaroni
  (I use large shells)
3 c. Thin White Sauce (recipe below)
1/2 to 1 lb. Cheddar cheese, grated

3 T. grated onion
1/2 tsp. dry mustard
1 tsp. Worcestershire sauce (opt.)
1/2 c. seasoned bread crumbs

Cook macaroni according to package; drain well. Combine heated white sauce, grated cheese, onion, dry mustard and Worcestershire sauce. Add to macaroni, reserving a little of the grated cheese. Top with bread crumbs, remaining cheese and a dash of paprika. Bake in a moderate oven (375°) for about 25 minutes, or until browned. Yield: 6 to 8 servings.

Freezes well.

THIN WHITE SAUCE:
5 T. butter
3 T. flour

1 tsp. salt
1/2 tsp. pepper
3 c. milk

Melt butter over low heat. Add flour, salt and pepper. Stir until well blended. Gradually stir in milk on low heat. Cook, stirring constantly, until thick and smooth. To shorten cooking time, milk may be heated separately. Yield: 3 cups, amount needed for recipe.

Lisa Bacchus Aronson

Macaroni and Cheese Casserole

1 (1 lb.) box cooked macaroni
2 eggs
1 1/2 c. milk
1 lb. shredded or cubed cheese
  (Cheddar works well)

1 med.-lg. chopped & sautéed
  onion
1 tsp. Crazy Jane (or regular)
  salt

Preheat oven to 350°. Mix the eggs, milk, cheese, onion and salt together. Grease a casserole pan. Place macaroni in casserole. Pour cheese mix over top. (Option: can place sliced onions, tomatoes and a little salt over top for a yummy topping. Can also mix chopped red peppers into the casserole for added flavor.) Bake at 350° for 30 minutes, uncovered.

Curt Huddleston

Vegetable Entrées
and Side Dishes

Ellen Metzger O'Shea
Diva Series, Corn
Oil on Paper

Cooking Times & Proportion for Grains & Beans

Grain (1 cup dry measure)	Water	Cooking Time	Yield
Barley (whole)	3 cups	1 hour 15 minutes	3 1/2 cups
Brown rice	2 cups	1 hour	3 cups
Buckwheat (kasha)	2 cups	15 minutes	2 1/2 cups
Bulgur wheat	2 cups	15-20 minutes	2 1/2 cups
Cracked wheat	2 cups	25 minutes	2 1/3 cups
Millet	3 cups	45 minutes	3 1/2 cups
Course cornmeal (polenta)	4 cups	25 minutes	3 cups
Wild rice	3 cups	1 hour or more	4 cups
Whole wheat berries	3 cups	2 hours	2 2/3 cups
Quinoa	2 cups	15 minutes	2 1/2 cups
Black beans	4 cups	1 1/2 hours	2 cups
Black-eyed peas	3 cups	1 hour	2 cups
Garbanzos (chickpeas)	4 cups	3 hours	2 cups
Great northern beans	3 1/2 cups	2 hours	2 cups
Kidney beans	3 cups	1 1/2 hours	2 cups
Lentils and split peas	3 cups	45 minutes	2 1/4 cups
Limas	2 cups	1 1/2 hours	1 1/4 cups
Baby limas	2 cups	1 1/2 hours	1 3/4 cups
Pinto beans	3 cups	2 1/2 hours	2 cups
Red beans	3 cups	3 hours	2 cups
Small white beans (navy, etc.)	3 cups	2 1/2 hours	2 cups
Soybeans	4 cups	3 hours or more	2 cups
Soy grits	2 cups	15 minutes	2 cups

To prepare dried beans, rinse them, picking them over to remove any pebbles. Place the beans in a large saucepan. Cover with boiling water by 2 inches. Cover and let stand until the beans swell to at least twice their size and have absorbed most of the liquid, about one hour. Drain beans in colander, discarding the soaking liquid.

Vegetable Entrées and Side Dishes

How to Stuff a Pepper

Now, said the cook, I will teach you
how to stuff a pepper with rice.

Take your pepper green, and gently,
for peppers are shy. No matter which side
you approach, it's always the backside.
Perched on green buttocks, the pepper sleeps.
In its silk tights, it dreams
of somersaults and parsley,
of the days when the sexes were one.

Slash open the sleeve
as if you were cutting a paper lantern,.
and enter a moon, spilled like a melon, ,
a fever of pearls,
a conversation of glaciers.
It is a temple built to the worship
of morning light.

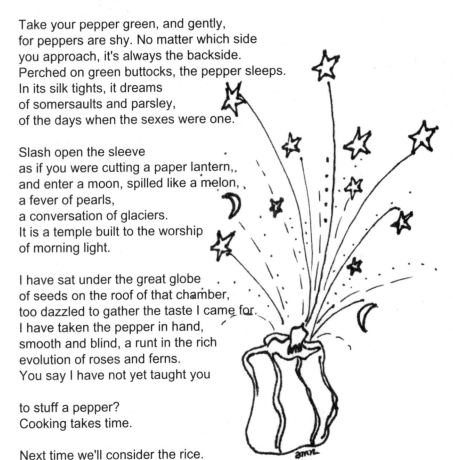

I have sat under the great globe
of seeds on the roof of that chamber,
too dazzled to gather the taste I came for.
I have taken the pepper in hand,
smooth and blind, a runt in the rich
evolution of roses and ferns.
You say I have not yet taught you

to stuff a pepper?
Cooking takes time.

Next time we'll consider the rice.
Nancy Willard

♥ Mexican Lasagna

1 sm. onion	1 (14 oz.) can black beans
1 c. red pepper	1/2 (1 lb.) can Worthington
3 c. eggplant	multi-grain cutlets, or 1
2 c. string beans	(12 oz.) pkg. Light Life Smart
2 c. greens (kale, spinach, etc.	ground meatless soy crumbs
2 T. fresh cilantro	6 to 8 corn tortillas
1/2 c. salsa	Cheddar cheese, grated (1 c. or
1 (14 oz.) can refried beans	more to taste) (opt.)

Preheat oven to 350°. Cut onion in half lengthwise and slice thin. Place in nonstick skillet with a little oil (or water – see comments); sauté. Slice red pepper, add to skillet and stir. Chop eggplant to bite-size pieces. Add to skillet; stir and add 1/4 cup salsa and cover. Chop string beans into bite-size pieces, add and stir and cover. Chop greens; add and stir and cover. Chop cilantro, add and stir. Cook until vegetables are tender (about 10 to 15 minutes total). In a separate pot, mix the refried beans, black beans and 1/4 cup salsa. Put on lowest heat and simmer for 10 to 15 minutes.

Spray bottom of 9x12-inch baking pan. Layer bottom with 3 to 4 corn tortillas, whatever it takes to cover the bottom of the pan. Spread bean mixture over corn tortillas. Sprinkle multi-grain cutlets, chopped into bite-size pieces, or Smart ground soy crumbles on top of beans. Place another layer of tortillas on top of that. Spread vegetable mixture on top of that. Sprinkle with grated cheese. Bake for 20 to 25 minutes. Remove from oven and let settle for 3 to 5 minutes. Cut and serve with salsa and salad.

No need to use oil to cook vegetables. In a nonstick skillet you can use water or wine instead. You can use an alternate combination of vegetables, anything goes. Use either 7 cups of vegetables or 6 cups of vegetables with 2 cups greens.

This is a vegetarian casserole which can be modified for you carnivores by substituting the vegetables or soy crumbles with ground beef or turkey. If you prefer a cheesier dish, put extra grated cheese on top of your bean layer as well.

Claudia Gorman

♥ Stuffed Butternut Squash

2 med.-size butternut squash
1 c. brown rice
1/4 c. quinoa
2 portobello mushrooms,
    chopped
2 cloves garlic, minced

1 sm. onion, chopped
1/2 c. peas
1 handful fresh spinach
Salt & pepper, to taste
1 c. shredded Cheddar cheese

Slice squash in half lengthwise and bake face-down in baking pan until soft in a 350° oven (about 40 minutes). Boil 2 1/2 cups vegetable broth or water. Add rice, garlic and onion and simmer, covered, for 10 minutes. Add quinoa and portobello mushrooms and simmer, covered, for 20 minutes. Add peas and spinach; simmer another 5 minutes, or until ready. When squash is ready, scoop out some of the flesh to make a cavity for the stuffing. Chop and add that squash to the rice mixture. Mix in 1/2 cup cheese, salt and pepper. Stuff squash. Sprinkle with remaining cheese and bake 20 minutes.

Using the quinoa adds another texture to the stuffing. If you would prefer, you can use 1 1/4 cups rice and omit quinoa.

You can add other vegetables. Try a red pepper or a zucchini.

Serve with soup or salad.

Ethel

♥ Stuffed Acorn Squash

1 med.-sized acorn squash	A pat of butter or margarine
2 sm. cooking apples (or 1 large)	Salt
	Lemon juice, to taste
2 T. cinnamon	1 tsp. dried basil
2 T. brown sugar	Chopped walnuts (opt.)

Set oven to 350°. Cut the squash in half. Scoop out the seeds and string stuff in the center. Fill a roasting pan half-full with water. Place the squash halves face-down in the water and bake for 30 minutes. While the squash is baking, peel and dice 2 cooking apples. Put the diced apples in a small bowl and coat with cinnamon. Add chopped walnuts, if desired.

After 30 minutes, remove the squash from the oven; flip over and put a dash of salt in the center. Fill center with the cinnamon-apples. Squeeze lemon juice on top of apples. Sprinkle with brown sugar and dot with a pat of butter or margarine. Sprinkle a sweet herb, such as basil, on top. Return to the oven for another 30 minutes. Squash is done when it is fork-tender. Serve hot. Yield: 2 servings.

Preparation and cooking time: approximately 1 hour.

Ruth Detjen

♥ Quick Curried Cauliflower

2 med. potatoes
1 lg. onion, chopped
1 med. head cauliflower
1 T. olive oil

1 (28 oz.) can tomatoes or
  Rienzi crushed tomatoes,
  peeled (preferable)
1 c. frozen Edamame shelled
  soybeans or frozen peas
1 c. whole wheat couscous
Feta cheese (opt.)

Spices to make your own curry, or use 2 to 2 1/2 tablespoons prepared curry:

1 tsp. ground ginger
1 T. ground cumin
1 tsp. ground cardamom
1 tsp. coriander
1/2 tsp. turmeric

1/8 tsp. cayenne pepper
1/2 tsp. mustard seeds
Salt & pepper, to taste
Fresh parsley (opt.)

Cut potatoes into bite-size pieces and boil until cooked but firm. Set aside. In large pan, sauté onion and cauliflower, cut into bite-size pieces, in oil, until onion is soft and cauliflower is lightly brown. Add spices and stir well; cook for 1 minute. Add crushed tomatoes, or if using whole tomatoes, chop them up and add. Cover and cook about 10 minutes. Add potatoes and soybeans or peas and cook until vegetables are the way you like them, 5 to 10 minutes. Add a handful of fresh chopped parsley. Serve over couscous and sprinkle with Feta cheese.

You can find Edamame soybeans in most health food stores.

For a higher protein meal, you can crack 2 eggs into pan about 5 minutes before ready. Stir. Or add a can of tuna when you add the potatoes.

Instead of parsley, you can use 1 to 2 cups fresh spinach, add when you add the potatoes.

Gertrude

Spinach and Potato Pie

2 1/2 lb. potatoes*
3 to 4 oz. butter
4 oz. milk
Salt & pepper, to taste
2 eggs, lightly beaten

4 to 6 oz. grated Parmesan
   cheese
2 lb. baby spinach
6 cloves crushed garlic
2 to 4 T. olive oil

Boil the potatoes in their skins until soft. Peel and mash them with a potato masher or fork. Add the butter, milk, salt, pepper, garlic and grated cheese, reserving 2 tablespoons. Mash and beat until smooth and well drained. Wash the spinach, drain, and press to get rid of excess water. Cook over low heat, covered, until leaves soften. They will steam in the moisture that clings to them. Season with salt and pepper.

In an oiled baking dish, spread half the mashed potatoes. Cover with the spinach, and then spread the remaining mashed potatoes. Sprinkle the remaining cheese and olive oil. Bake at 400° for about 40 minutes, or until lightly golden. Yield: 6 servings.

*I found 8 to 9 medium-size potatoes worked well.

This was wonderful side dish for a dairy meal during Passover.

Bacchus Aronson

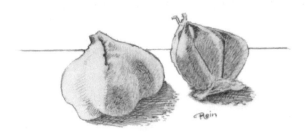

♥ Helen's Baked Tofu

1 lb. firm tofu
2 to 3 T. lemon juice
1 1/2 T. olive oil
1 T. tamari soy sauce

2 T. fresh rosemary, tarragon or
   other herbs, or smaller amount
   of dried herbs
White pepper, to taste (opt.)

Slice tofu in 1/4-inch slices; place in shallow baking dish. Mix other ingredients together. Pour over tofu. Bake for 45 minutes at 350°. Yield: 4 servings.

Variations: Use 1/2 the tofu with more than 1/2 the sauce – serves 2. Use balsamic vinegar instead of lemon juice. Or try tomatoes, mashed, and experiment with seasonings. I always add some grated fresh garlic. Fresh grated ginger is also good. Almost anything goes, don't be afraid to be creative! I found that it works better with more sauce. I like to broil it when it's almost done.

Make it a few hours before baking to marinate!

Margaret Crenson

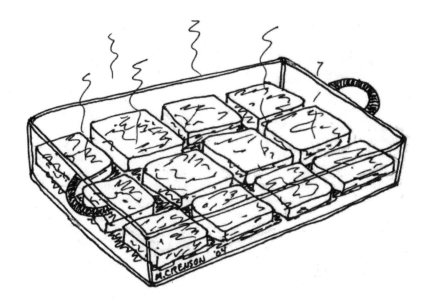

♥ Mushroom Burgers

1 lb. portobello mushrooms	1/2 lb. silken tofu, mashed
1 sm. onion	3 egg whites, or 1 egg & 1 white
3 cloves garlic, minced	1 T. tamari soy sauce
1/4 c. wine (red or white)	Salt & pepper, to taste
Olive oil	1 c. cooked rice (preferably brown)
Cheddar cheese or tahini (opt.)	1/2 c. (or more) fresh bread crumbs

Chop mushrooms and onions into small pieces. Place in saucepan with garlic and wine. Cook until mushrooms are soft. Simmer, covered, about 10 minutes, then 5 minutes without lid, to cook off liquid. While this is cooking, in a bowl, mix tofu, eggs, soy sauce, salt and pepper, and rice. Add mushroom mixture; stir. Gradually add enough bread crumbs to create a consistency that can be made into patties. Fry patties in a little bit of oil, about 5 minutes on each side. You can melt some cheese on top or serve with tahini. Yield: 8 burgers.

Claudia Gorman

Roasted Exotic Mushrooms
(Great with steak or fillets)

2 garlic cloves	1/2 lb. shiitake mushrooms
1/2 bunch flat-leaf parsley	(most any combination of
1/4 c. + 1 T. extra-virgin olive	exotic mushrooms may be used)
oil	2 T. clarified butter
1/2 lb. oyster mushrooms	Juice from 1/2 lemon
1/2 lb. chanterelle mushrooms	Kosher or sea salt
	Freshly-ground pepper

Preheat the oven to 475°. Finely chop the garlic in a food processor. Scrape sides of bowl down, add the parsley and finely chop. Slowly add 1/4 cup of the oil. Scrape down the sides of the bowl and then pulse the machine to make a fairly fine mixture but keeping some texture. Do not make it a smooth texture. Trim the mushrooms, discarding the stems of the shiitake but keeping the others. Halve or quarter the mushrooms in uniform pieces. Heat the clarified butter and remaining tablespoon of oil in a large skillet that can hold all the mushrooms. Add the mushrooms and toss over high heat 3 to 4 minutes, or until they wilt. Sprinkle the lemon juice over them. Transfer them to a shallow roasting pan, add parsley mixture and roast in the oven for 15 minutes. Remove from oven and season with salt and pepper. Serve. Yield: 4 to 6 servings.

Carol McGinnis

Braised Fennel with a Mushroom Cream Sauce

1 bulb fennel per person	Wine (opt.)
1 (14 oz.) can vegetable broth	1/2 c. sweet bread crumbs

MUSTARD CREAM SAUCE:

1/2 c. extra-strong Dijon	1 tsp. coriander seeds
mustard	1 c. sour cream
1/2 c. sweet mustard	1/2 c. golden raisins

Preheat oven to 350°. Slice fennel in half, remove ends with filigree so only bulb and stalk remain. Wash to remove grit. Lay fennel in Pyrex baking pan. Cover with vegetable broth and a touch of white wine (optional). Bake, covered with foil, with holes punched in it. Bake until tender, but firm.

Mix together cream sauce ingredients until creamy. Pour over cooked fennel and top with raisins. Continue to cook fennel until absolutely buttery soft! When done, cover with bread crumbs and broil until golden. Voila!

Bi Bi De Felice

♥ Lemon Lentils

1 c. lentils, rinsed & picked	1/4 c. olive oil
over	1/2 c. lemon juice (or 1/4 c.
4 c. water	lemon & 1/4 c. lime)
1 c. chopped fresh cilantro	1 garlic clove, minced & mashed
1 1/2 c. Swiss chard or	1 T. flour
spinach	2 tsp. salt
1/2 c. chopped onion	1 lg. potato, cut into 1/2" dice

In saucepan, combine lentils with 4 cups water; bring water to a boil and simmer, covered, for 20 minutes. Stir in cilantro and chard. In skillet, cook onion in oil 6 minutes; add it to lentil mixture and bring to a simmer. In small bowl, combine lemon juice, garlic, flour and salt; stir into lentil mixture. Add potato and continue to simmer mixture until potato is tender. Yield: 8 servings.

Karla Nihal

♥ Roasted Root Vegetables

3 parsnips
3 potatoes
3 carrots
2 sweet potatoes
1 sweet onion
2 garlic cloves

1/4 c. olive oil
2 T. mustard seed
Rosemary
Salt & pepper
2 T. balsamic vinegar

Preheat oven to 375°. Bring a saucepan of lightly-salted water to a boil. Cube vegetables (except onion and garlic) and boil for 2 minutes. Drain thoroughly. On top of stove in a heavy roasting pan, heat 1/4 cup of olive oil. Add cut-up onion and garlic cloves; sauté gently a few minutes. Add vegetables and sauté, until golden at the edges, stirring them in the pan. Add seasoning of 2 teaspoons mustard seed, some coarse salt and fresh rosemary, if available. Add 2 tablespoons balsamic vinegar. Roast in oven about 45 minutes, or until tender and golden, stirring occasionally.

Kay Moore

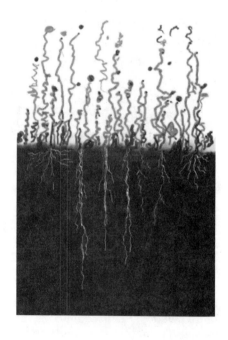

♥ Carrots with Tarragon

**8 carrots, cleaned, peeled
& sliced in rounds
1 T. chopped fresh tarragon**

**Juice from 1/2 lemon
Salt, to taste
Butter (opt.)**

Place carrots in boiling water, approximately 2-inches high, with tarragon, and cook until just tender, approximately 5 to 10 minutes, depending on size. Strain and toss with lemon juice, salt and butter, if desired.

Laurie Bloomfield

♥ Asparagus with Orange Sauce

**2 lb. fresh asparagus, trimmed
1/4 c. plain nonfat yogurt
2 T. light mayonnaise
Orange slices & additional
peel (opt.)**

**2 T. orange juice
1 tsp. grated orange peel
Dash of cayenne pepper**

Place the asparagus and a little water in a skillet; bring to boil. Cook for 6 to 8 minutes, or until crisp-tender. Meanwhile, combine yogurt, mayonnaise, juice, peel and cayenne pepper. Drain asparagus; top with orange sauce. Garnish with orange slices and peel, if desired. Yield: 8 servings.

Joanne Vanderveer

Senator Russell's Sweet Potatoes

4 to 6 sweet potatoes, peeled
  & boiled (or 2 lg. cans),
  mashed
1 c. sugar

1 tsp. vanilla
1/2 c. margarine
2 eggs
1/2 c. milk

TOPPING:
1 c. brown sugar
1 c. chopped pecans

1/4 c. flour
1/3 c. margarine

Mix potatoes, sugar, vanilla, margarine, eggs and milk. Spread in 10x13-inch shallow buttered dish. Spread on topping. Bake at 350° for 30 minutes. Yield: 12 servings.

Marie Dill

♥ Basmati Rice

2 T. chopped shallots
2 T. chopped fresh parsley
1 tsp. crushed lemon thyme

1 c. basmati rice
1 3/4 c. chicken broth
1 bay leaf

Sauté shallots, parsley and lemon thyme for approximately 2 minutes on medium flame. Add rice and coat with mixture. Add chicken broth and bay leaf; bring to a boil. Reduce heat. Cover and simmer for approximately 25 minutes, or until liquid is absorbed.

Laurie Bloomfield

♥ Creole Orange Rice

2 T. nonhydrogenated
    margarine
1 lg. onion, finely chopped
2 lg. celery stalks, diced
1 1/3 c. long-grain brown rice
2 c. homemade vegetable
    stock, or 1 (15 oz.) can
1 c. fresh orange juice

1 tsp. grated orange zest (opt.)
1/4 tsp. dried thyme
Salt & freshly-ground pepper
Minced parsley, for garnish
Peeled & sectioned clementine
    or other small seedless
    oranges, for garnish (opt.)

Heat the butter in a large saucepan. Add the onion and celery; sauté over medium heat until the onion is golden. Add the rice, stock, orange juice, optional orange zest and thyme, plus 1 cup water. Bring to a simmer, then simmer gently, covered, until the water is absorbed, about 20 minutes.

If the rice is not tender enough for your taste, add another 1/2 cup water and simmer until absorbed. Season to taste with salt and pepper. Serve at once. Garnish each serving with a little minced parsley and, if desired, a few clementine sections. Yield: 6 servings.

Adapted from "Great American Vegetarian" by **Nava Atlas**.

♥ Hearty Mixed Grain Pilaf

1/2 c. bulgur
1/2 c. quinoa
2 c. water or vegetable broth
1 c. sweet red peppers,
    chopped

1 scallion, finely chopped
2 mushrooms, sliced
1/2 c. peas
2 T. salsa, mild or spicy, your
    choice

Boil 2 cups water in 3-quart saucepan. Add quinoa, bulgur, sweet pepper, mushrooms, scallions and peas. Return to boil, lower heat and cover. Simmer 18 minutes. Add salsa and stir (liquid should be gone and grains should be soft). Let rest for 5 minutes, covered. Yield: 4 to 6 servings as side dish.

Cassie Chu

♥ Barley with Mushrooms and Browned Onions

The darker mushrooms yield a richer flavor, so give them a try. As always, my favorite seasoning for barley is fresh dill.

1 c. pearl or pot barley	8 to 10 oz. cremini, baby bella
1 1/2 T. light olive oil	or white mushrooms
2 lg. onions, quartered &	2 to 3 T. minced fresh dill
thinly sliced	Salt & freshly-ground pepper, to taste

Bring 3 cups water to a rapid simmer in a medium saucepan and stir in the barley. Cover and simmer gently until the water is absorbed, about 35 to 40 minutes. Taste, and if you'd like a little more tender texture, add another 1/2 cup water and simmer until absorbed.

Meanwhile, heat the oil in a wide skillet. Add the onions and sauté slowly over low heat until lightly and evenly browned. Add the mushrooms and about 1/4 cup of water. Cover and cook over medium heat until the mushrooms are wilted, about 8 minutes. Combine the onion and mushroom mixture with the cooked barley in a serving container. Stir in the dill, season with salt and pepper and serve. Yield: 4 to 6 servings.

Adapted from "The Vegetarian 5-Ingredient Gourmet" by **Nava Atlas**.

♥ Lemony Green Beans

1 1/4 lb. green beans, trimmed	2 tsp. fresh lemon juice
2 tsp. olive oil	1/2 tsp. salt
1 c. sliced shallots	1/2 tsp. black pepper
1 tsp. grated lemon rind	

Place beans in large saucepan of boiling water. Cook 5 minutes, or until crisp-tender; drain. Plunge beans into ice water; drain and set aside.

Heat oil in nonstick skillet over medium heat. Add shallots; sauté 5 minutes, or until golden. Add green beans, lemon rind and lemon juice. Cook 2 minutes, stirring occasionally. Remove from heat. Stir in salt and pepper.

James Ransome,
Lesa Cline-Ransome

Sauces,
Dressings and Salsas

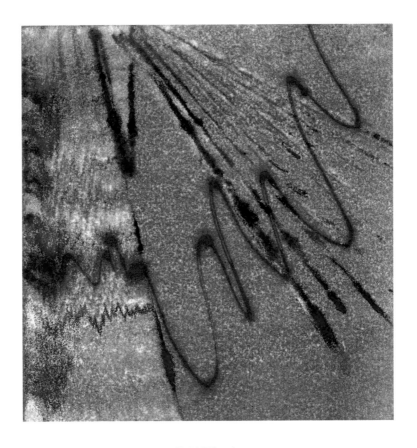

Enid Watsky
Celebration
Monoprint

Gardening & Houseplant Hints

- Plant onions next to carrots to prevent carrot worms.
- When your hands are badly stained from gardening, add a teaspoon of sugar to the soapy lather you wash them in.
- Cut old stockings lengthwise to make ties for tomato plants. These will not cut into the stalk, and are very strong. They also work great for tying up cauliflower.
- Plant a few sprigs of dill near your tomato plants to prevent tomato worms on your plants.
- To remove poison ivy, mix a gallon of soapy water and 3 pounds of salt and spray the area.
- Marigolds will prevent rodents.
- Spray cut flowers with hair spray to make them last longer.
- Use a salt shaker to sow small seeds in your garden — it will distribute the seeds more evenly.
- Pour boiling salted water on grass or weeds growing between sections of sidewalk or use cheap motor oil.
- Add a teaspoon of sugar to the water in vases of marigolds to remove their strong smell.
- Plants may fail if the water is too cold or hot — use room temperature or warm water. Melted snow is very good for the plants.
- You can give added light to indoor plants by setting the pot on foil or placing foil in back of the plants to reflect sunlight.
- A tablespoon of castor oil chased by water brings sick plants out of their slump.
- Swab plant leaves with a few drops of glycerine on a cloth for a glossy shine.
- Sprinkle moth crystals around in your vegetables and flower garden to keep animals such as rabbits, chipmunks and dogs out. If you have problems with small animals eating your plants, just sprinkle with red pepper powder.
- Don't throw away your leftover coffee in the morning. Pour it around your geraniums to promote blooming.
- Your African violets will bloom longer, prettier and more abundantly, if you stick a few rusty nails in the soil alongside them.
- A potato buried beside the root of a newly set out plant provides moisture and nutrition to help the plant get started. Be sure to take the eyes out of the potato, or you'll have a potato crop, too. Peels work too.
- A geranium cutting can be started easily by boring a hole in a potato and placing the cut end of stem in the potato and planting the potato in soil.

Sauces, Dressings and Salsas

♥ Lemon Soy Barbecue Sauce

2 lemons
4 T. tamari soy sauce

4 T. Dijon mustard
1 T. oil (opt.)

Squeeze lemons. Should get about 6 tablespoons juice. Mix all ingredients together; stir well.
Great on seafood, vegetables, meats and poultry.

Sadie Wertzheiser

♥ Mushroom Sauce

3/4 lb. mushrooms, finely
   chopped
1/2 c. white wine
1 c. vegetable broth
1/2 tsp. thyme or marjoram
   or basil

1 sliced scallion
2 1/2 T. cornstarch, dissolved
   in 2 T. cold water
1 1/2 T. tamari soy sauce
Fresh black pepper, to taste

In a saucepan, bring mushrooms to a boil in the wine and vegetable broth. Add scallion and herb of your choice. Simmer 10 to 15 minutes. Whisk in the cornstarch and stir continuously until gravy thickens. Add soy sauce and pepper.
This sauce is good over mixed vegetables, potatoes or pasta, and probably many other things!

Sadie Wertzheiser

If mushrooms are gritty, blanch them in salted water for 3 minutes, then rinse under cold running water and drain.

♥ Oriental Sauce for Stir-Fry

3/4 c. water or vegetable broth
4 cloves garlic, minced
1 T. orange juice
2 T. rice wine vinegar

1/4 c. tamari soy sauce (or more
   to taste)
2 heaping T. cornstarch,
   dissolved in 1/4 c. cold water

Boil water or vegetable broth and garlic. Simmer 3 minutes. Add orange juice and vinegar; stir. Add 1/4 cup tamari soy sauce and cornstarch dissolved in water. Lower heat and stir until thick. Pour over your stir-fry. Makes little over 1 cup.

Sadie Wertzheiser

♥ Marinara Sauce a la Lou's Mama

Puddle of olive oil
6 cloves garlic
1 lg. white onion
4 cans Italian plum tomatoes
4 cans Contadina tomato paste

Black pepper, to taste
Dried basil, to taste
Thyme, to taste
Red pepper, to taste

In a big pot, put a puddle of olive oil. Mince garlic. Fry up the garlic in the oil, don't burn. Chop onion; put into pot and caramelize. Dump in Italian plum tomatoes and Contadina tomato paste. Bring to boil, stir regularly. Don't allow to burn. If burns, change pots – don't scrape. Do not cook too long. Plum tomatoes should become tender and will break easily in pot with fork or wooden spoon. Seasoning includes crushed black pepper, basil, dried, crushed, (lots of) thyme. Test to taste. Powdered red pepper for zip. My sauce is never the same twice.

My friend Lou gave me this recipe. I have made it many times. I use much more garlic than he does. The plum tomatoes are the large 35-ounce-size with juice. The tomato paste I use is the 6-ounce-size and any brand. Sometimes I cut up some of the tomatoes before I put them in the big pot. After I bring the sauce to a boil, I simmer and stir often. Sauce takes about 1/2 hour to make. Sauce makes about 16-plus cups and freezes very well. It is my favorite marinara sauce.

Lisa Bacchus Aronson

♥ Vegetable Tomato Sauce

1 med.-lg. onion, chopped
6 cloves garlic, finely chopped
1 carrot, minced
2 (28 oz.) cans Rienzi crushed
   tomatoes, peeled (or any
   brand cut into bite-size
   pieces)
1 (28 oz.) can tomato purée
1 (6 oz.) can tomato paste
1/4 lb. mushrooms (portobello
   works well), finely chopped

1 sm. eggplant
1/2 c. fresh basil, if not
   available, combine the
   following dry herbs: 1 T. basil,
   2 tsp. thyme, 2 tsp. oregano
1/2 tsp. pepper (or more to
   taste)
Salt, to taste
1/2 c. wine (opt.)
Olive oil

Peel eggplant, slice lengthwise in half. Coat lightly with olive oil. Place face-down on baking dish. Slice lengthwise (again) into 1-inch slices. Roast in oven at 375° until tender, about 15 minutes. Cut into 1-inch chunks. Sauté onion in a little oil in 5-quart saucepan for 5 minutes. Add garlic; sauté 3 minutes. Add carrot and tomato products and mushrooms. Bring to gentle boil, lower heat and simmer, uncovered (or with lid ajar) 1 hour, stirring occasionally. Add herbs, spices, eggplant and wine, and cook an additional 1/2 hour, stirring occasionally, or until desired thickness. Makes a little more than 3 quarts.

Freezes well.

The minced carrot sweetens the sauce.

Mary Jane

Thai Dressing

3 T. lime juice
2 T. rice wine vinegar
3 T. peanut butter
1 tsp. ginger (fresh grated)
1/4 to 1/2 tsp. red chilies

2 T. soy sauce
1 tsp. honey
1 T. fresh cilantro, chopped
2 T. water

Mix all. Chill.

Great on salads, warm vegetables, seafood and many other things!

Rachael Robbins

Grainy Mustard Vinaigrette

1/3 c. canola oil
3 T. olive oil
1/3 c. red or white wine vinegar
Juice of 1/2 lemon
2 to 3 T. grainy mustard, to taste
1 clove garlic, crushed (opt.)

1/2 tsp. dried dill
1/4 tsp. dried tarragon
1/4 tsp. savory
1/4 tsp. basil
Freshly-ground black pepper, to taste

Combine all the ingredients in a cruet and shake well. Shake well before each use. Yield: about 1 cup.

Adapted from "Vegetarian Celebrations" by **Nava Atlas**.

French Dressing

Make this dressing at least an hour before it is needed. It can also be made several days ahead of time, as it keeps well under refrigeration.

1/3 c. tomato juice
1/4 c. light olive oil
2 T. red wine vinegar
1 T. + 1 tsp. reduced-fat mayonnaise or soy mayonnaise

2 tsp. honey or light brown sugar
1 tsp. paprika
Freshly-ground pepper, to taste
1 to 2 cloves garlic, split lengthwise

Combine all ingredients in a small mixing bowl and whisk together until smoothly combined. Use garlic according to how garlicky you like dressings – 2 cloves steeped in the dressing for a day or more will produce a fairly pungent garlic flavor.

Transfer to a covered container or cruet and refrigerate until needed. Yield: about 1 cup.

Adapted from "Vegetarian Celebrations" by **Nava Atlas**.

♥ M. G. Wells' Speedy Tomato Salsa

64 oz. Pace mild picante sauce
   or any brand you like*
1 or 2 chopped, seeded
   jalapeño or green chili
   peppers (depends on how
   hot you like it!)
1 ample bunch of fresh cilantro**

2 T. fresh lime juice
2 T. fresh lemon juice (the
   lemon/lime squeezers are
   good too)
1/8 tsp. sea salt (or more to
   your personal taste)

For a Zesty Southwestern version, add:

1 (16 oz.) can crispy, canned
   corn, drained & washed (opt.)

1 (16 oz.) can black beans,
   drained & washed (opt.)

*Pace is my favorite because they don't add refined sugar.
**Use the stems too because they are crunchy, flavorful and packed with healthy nutrients!

Chop all ingredients by hand or use a food processor. Either way is just great so lets get going! Thoroughly wash cilantro in a colander, shake excess water and let drain in sink. Carefully cut and scrape the seeds from your chili peppers and promptly rinse with cool water. Do not touch your face, eyes or mouth until you wash your hands as the chili oil is hot. Pour salsa into food processor or bowl. Fill salsa jar with 1/4 cup water, replace lid and shake well. Pour remaining salsa/water into your food processor or bowl. Mix your fantastic concoction, place all in an ample container and chill. (I use a plastic pitcher since I find it makes the salsa easier to serve.)

Serve with tortilla chips, any Mexican food, cucumber, eggs or anything you like! Yield: enough for 20 hungry people, maybe more. May be stored in refrigerator for at least a month.

Enjoy!

M.G. Wells

To cool down a dish with too much chili pepper, add a dairy product (cheese, yogurt, sour cream) or some sugar. You can also add chunks of raw potato to absorb some of the chilies capsaicin. If none of these work, make a second batch without the chili and mix it with the first batch.

♥ Salsa Ranchera
(Fresh Tomato Salsa)

2 c. chopped ripe tomatoes,
  or 1 (14 to 16 oz.) can
  diced tomatoes, lightly drained
1 sm. onion, quartered
1 (4 oz.) can chopped mild
  green chilies

1 to 2 fresh jalapeño peppers,
  seeded & coarsely chopped
  (opt.)
Several sprigs fresh cilantro
1 T. lemon juice
1/2 tsp. cumin
1/4 tsp. salt (or to taste)

To prepare in a food processor, simply combine all the ingredients in the work bowl and pulse on and off until the ingredients are coarsely puréed. To prepare by hand, finely chop the tomatoes, onion, optional jalapeños and cilantro. Stir in the remaining ingredients. Store in an airtight jar. Yield: about 2 cups.

This will keep for several days, but is best fresh.

Adapted from "Great American Vegetarian" by **Nava Atlas**.

♥ M. G.'s Hawaiian Delight Salsa

1 c. finely-chopped fresh or
  canned (in water) pineapple
  (if you use canned, save 1/3
  of pineapple water for mix)
1 c. chopped, peeled mango
1 c. chopped, peeled papaya
1 c. coarsely-chopped red or
  orange bell pepper, or both!

1/2 c. chopped red onion
1/3 c. minced fresh cilantro
1 T. lime juice
1 T. lemon juice
1 med. chopped, seeded mild
  green chili

Mix all ingredients in a bowl. Cover and chill for 2 hours. Yield: 4 cups. Serve with tortilla chips, your favorite crackers or fresh vegetables.

M.G. Wells

♥ Santa Fe Cranberry Relish

1 (12 oz.) pkg. fresh
  cranberries
1 med. jalapeño pepper,
  quartered & seeded

3/4 c. sugar
1 scallion, quartered
1 tsp. chopped fresh cilantro
1/4 tsp. cumin

Combine all in food processor until coarsely chopped. Store overnight, refrigerated, to meld flavors before serving.

Great accompaniment to roast turkey.

Dan Hogan

♥ Grandma Stowell's No-Cook Cranberry Relish

1 lb. cranberries
2 apples

2 California oranges, keep rind of 1
Sugar

Grind cranberries, apples and oranges in hand grinder. Add 1 cup sugar per 1 cup relish. Refrigerate overnight.

Nancy McKenna

♥ Cucumber Raita

Raitas are yogurt-based salads that provide a refreshing contrast to spicy dishes.

2 lg. cucumbers, peeled, seeded & chopped
1 1/2 c. plain low-fat yogurt or soy yogurt

2 to 3 T. chopped fresh cilantro or parsley
2 T. minced fresh mint, or 1 tsp. dried mint
1/2 tsp. ground cumin

Combine all the ingredients in a mixing bowl. Chill before serving, then transfer to a serving container. Yield: 6 to 8 servings.
Adapted from "Vegetarian Celebrations" by **Nava Atlas**.

♥ Aglione Rub for Chicken

2 T. olive oil
1 T. chopped fresh rosemary

1 clove garlic, coarsely chopped
1 tsp. salt

Combine all ingredients, rub mixture all over chicken, both inside and out. Cover and refrigerate overnight. When you are ready to cook chicken, remove large pieces of garlic and rosemary.

Marinate chicken in rub overnight.

Lisa Aronson

*"Sauces are to cookery what the gamut is to the composition of music,
as it is by the arrangement of notes that harmony is produced,
so should the ingredients in the sauce by nicely blended,
and that delightful concord should exist, which would equally delight the palate,
as a masterpiece of a Mozart or a Rossini should delite the ear."*
Alexis Soyer (1851)

Desserts

Helene Small
Still Life with Fruit
Pastel on Sanded Paper

Long time members will remember the annual holiday bazaar each December when Barrett House would be turned into a shopper's paradise. One of the most popular parts of this yearly event was "Betty's Kitchen" where baked goods would be sold. Nini's Cheesecake was always a hit but the recipe was never shared despite numerous requests. Now, for the first time, you too can enjoy this simple but delicious dessert.

Wayne Lempka

Desserts

Nini's Holiday Bazaar Cheesecake

2 (8 oz.) pkg. cream cheese,
   softened
2 pt. (32 oz.) sour cream
3 eggs

1 c. sugar
2 to 3 tsp. vanilla
1/4 tsp. salt
8 or more graham crackers, crushed

On the bottom of a 10-inch springform pan, place the crushed graham crackers so that the surface is covered and is approximately 1/4-inch thick. Beat eggs, sugar and salt together. Add cream cheese gradually and beat thoroughly. Add sour cream and vanilla; beat again. Pour into the springform pan and bake at 350° for 1 hour, or until knife comes out clean from center. Cool and enjoy with a cup of freshly-brewed Earl Gray tea.

Wayne Lempka

Sarah Livingston's Poppyseed Cake

3/4 c. poppyseeds
3/4 c. milk
1/2 c. butter or margarine
3/4 c. sugar
2 c. flour

3 tsp. baking powder
1/2 tsp. salt
1 tsp. vanilla
4 egg whites

Mix poppy seeds and heated milk.
   In a separate bowl, cream butter and sugar. Sift in flour, baking powder and salt.
   In a separate bowl, beat egg whites until stiff. Mix together. Pour into 8x8-inch greased pan. Bake at 350° for 45 minutes.

Angel Gingerbread

1/4 c. butter
1/2 c. sugar
1 egg
1/4 c. molasses
1 c. flour
1 tsp. ginger

1 tsp. baking soda
1/4 tsp. cloves
1/4 tsp. cinnamon
1/4 tsp. salt
1/2 c. water

Combine all ingredients, adding the water last. Pour into 8-inch greased pan. Bake in 350° oven for 25 minutes.

Joanne Rein

Louise Spencer's Butter Cake
(Stacie's Almond Wedding Cake)

6 c. sifted cake flour
4 tsp. baking powder
1 1/2 tsp. salt
2 c. butter
3 1/2 c. granulated sugar

6 eggs
2 egg yolks
1 1/2 c. milk
2 tsp. almond extract
2 tsp. vanilla extract

Sift flour, baking powder and salt together; set aside.

In a large bowl, cream butter and add sugar gradually; beat well. Add eggs, egg yolks and both extracts. Continue to beat until very light and fluffy. Reduce mixer speed to low. Add dry ingredients in 5 portions, alternating with milk, beating only enough to blend after each addition.

Grease and flour cake pans. Line with waxed paper if desired. Fill with batter to 1/2 full. Bake at 350° (or store in refrigerator up to 3 hours before baking): 8- and 10-inch cake pans will bake for 25 to 30 minutes; 12-inch pans take about 45 minutes. Cool in pans on a rack for 10 minutes. Turn out of pans to cool about 1 hour. Yield: 12 cups batter.

Chocolate Almond Midnight

CASHEW CRUST:
1/3 c. cashews
3 T. sucanat or sugar
3 T. canola oil or more to ball up
   crust

1/2 tsp. vanilla
1 c. flour
1/8 tsp. salt

CHOCOLATE MOUSSE:
2 c. malt sweetened nondairy
   chocolate chips
24.6 oz. extra-firm low-fat
   silken tofu

3/4 c. sucanat
1 tsp. vanilla
1/8 tsp. salt

MAPLE ALMOND PRALINE:
1/4 c. maple syrup

1 c. slivered almonds

RASPBERRY SAUCE:
12 oz. (more or less) frozen or
   fresh raspberries

Sucanat, for sweetening, if necessary

Crust: Preheat oven to 350°. Lightly oil an 8-inch round springform or false-bottom pan. In a food processor, grind the cashews until they resemble fine meal. Add the sucanat, oil and vanilla. Process again until well combined. In a small bowl, stir the flour and salt together. Add the cashew mixture and mix into the flour, beginning with a spatula and ending with your hands. Press the crust into the prepared pan. Bake for 20 to 25 minutes, or until light brown and dry.

Mousse: In a double boiler over barely simmering water, melt the chocolate chips. In a blender or processor, combine the silken tofu, sucanat, vanilla and salt. Process, then add melted chocolate and blend for 2 minutes, or until very smooth and completely combined. In a heated 350° oven, pour mousse mixture into prepared pan and bake for 35 minutes. Let cool for 10 minutes, then run a paring knife around the inside of the pan. Let the cake cool to the touch, refrigerate for at least 2 hours before serving. Unmold just before serving.

Praline: In a heavy-bottomed saucepan, bring the maple syrup to a boil. Boil for 1 minute, add the almonds and stir constantly until the syrup has completely crystallized onto the almonds and the almonds appear dry. Pour the almonds onto a baking sheet and let cool.

To serve, cut the cake into 12 pieces. For each serving, pool raspberry sauce on a plate and top with a slice of cake. Top with 1 tablespoon praline and garnish with fresh fruit, cocoa powder and mint. Yield: 12 servings.

Sucanat is the tops and leaves of the sugar cane plant and can be found at most health food stores.
                                                         Markey's Mom

Chocolate Yogurt Cake

1 1/2 c. all-purpose flour
3/4 tsp. baking powder
Pinch of fine sea salt
3 lg. eggs
1 c. sugar
1/2 c. plain yogurt

1 tsp. vanilla
8 T. unsalted butter, melted & cooled
3 oz. bitter chocolate, melted in
   double boiler, then cooled
Confectioners' sugar (opt.)

Butter and flour 1 (9 1/2-inch) round cake pan. Preheat the oven to 375°. Sift together the flour, baking powder and salt.

In a large bowl, whisk together the eggs and the sugar until they are light and pale yellow. Sprinkle the dry ingredients over the eggs and sugar, whisking to incorporate them. Fold in the yogurt and vanilla, then the melted butter.

Pour half the batter into the prepared cake pan. Fold the melted chocolate into the remaining batter until it is thoroughly combined. Pour the chocolate batter on top of the plain batter that is already in the cake pan and run a rubber spatula through the batter several times to make a marble pattern.

Bake for 35 minutes. Check to see if done by gently touching top, your finger should leave a slight impression. Remove cake from oven and let cool for about 15 minutes. Turn it out onto a cooling rack to fully cool. Dust with confectioners' sugar.

Joanne VanDerveer

Cream Cheese Cookies

1 c. sugar
1 (4 oz.) pkg. cream cheese
1 c. butter
1/2 tsp. lemon rind, grated

1 tsp. baking powder
3 1/2 c. flour
1 tsp. lemon juice

Cream butter and sugar; add cream cheese, juice and rind. Add flour, sifted with baking powder. Shape into 2 rolls; cover with waxed paper. Chill in refrigerator overnight. Slice thin. Bake at 350° for 10 minutes, or until edges are brown.

Vera Munson

Sugar and Spice Cookies

3/4 c. soft butter
1 c. sugar
1 egg
1/4 c. molasses
2 c. sifted flour

2 tsp. baking soda
1/4 tsp. salt
1 tsp. cinnamon
3/4 tsp. ground cloves
3/4 tsp. ground ginger

Cream first 4 ingredients. Sift together dry ingredients. Stir into creamed mixture and blend well. Form balls and place 2 inches apart on greased cookie sheet. Bake at 375° for 10 to 12 minutes. Roll in confectioners' sugar while still warm.

Elayne Seaman

"Hudson Valley Cookies in bloom"

Nut-Apricot Sticks

1/2 c. butter
1/2 c. sugar
1 tsp. grated lemon rind
2 egg whites
1 (10 oz.) jar apricot jam
2 egg yolks

1 c. flour
1 tsp. salt
1/2 tsp. baking soda
1 c. finely-chopped nuts (walnuts)
1 tsp. sugar

Preheat oven to 350°. Cream together the butter, sugar and rind. Add egg yolks, flour, salt and baking soda. Spread on greased shallow 8x12-inch pan. Cover batter with apricot preserves. Beat egg whites until stiff, but not dry. Add 1 teaspoon sugar, fold in finely-chopped walnuts. Spread over apricots. Bake at 350° for 45 minutes. Cut into strips. Serve warm.

Diane Robbins

Maya's Death by Chocolate Cookies

2 pkg. (16 sq.) Baker's semi-sweet
  chocolate, divided
3/4 c. brown sugar
1/4 c. butter or margarine
2 eggs
1 tsp. vanilla
1/2 c. flour
1/4 tsp. baking powder
2 c. chopped nuts

Heat oven to 350°. Chop 8 squares of the chocolate; set aside. Microwave remaining 8 squares on HIGH for 1 to 2 minutes. Stir until chocolate is melted and smooth. Stir in butter, eggs and vanilla. Stir in flour and baking powder. Stir in chopped chocolate and nuts. Drop by 1/4 cupfuls onto ungreased cookie sheet. Bake 12 to 13 minutes, or until cookies are puffed and soft to touch. Cool on cookie sheet 1 minute. Transfer to wire rack and cool. Yield: about 1 1/2 dozen cookies.

James Ransome and Lesa Cline-Ransome

Cindy Dill's No Milk or Chocolate Low-Wheat Cookies

3/4 c. quinoa flour & 1/4 c. almond
  flour & 1 c. wheat flour
2 1/2 c. oatmeal flour
1 tsp. baking soda
1 tsp. baking powder
1/2 tsp. salt
1 c. sugar
1 c. brown sugar
1 tsp. cinnamon
1 c. soy margarine
1 tsp. vanilla
2 eggs
1 1/2 c. chopped nuts
1 1/2 c. dry cranberries or raisins
  or coconut

Cream margarine and both sugars. Add eggs and vanilla; mix well. Mix dry ingredients, except nuts and fruits.

Mix flour and margarine mixes together. Add nuts and fruits. Place tablespoon-size balls on ungreased cookie sheet 2 inches apart. Bake 13 minutes at 375°. Yield: 65.

Cindy Dill

Bob's Red Mill Almond Cookies

1 c. oat flour, sifted
1 c. almond flour
1/2 c. butter

6 T. maple syrup or light brown
  sugar
1 tsp. vanilla
Cinnamon & sugar, for dusting

Cream butter, sugar and vanilla. Add almond flour and oat flour; mix until the dough sticks together. Form into 1 1/2-inch balls. Place on greased cookie sheet. Bake at 300° for 30 to 35 minutes. Roll cookies while warm, in cinnamon-sugar. Yield: 24.

Pumpkin Pie

2 c. butternut squash, steamed or
  baked, peeled & mashed
1/2 c. honey, or less (butternut
  squash is quite sweet)
1 tsp. cinnamon
1/2 tsp. ginger

1/4 tsp. nutmeg
1 c. liquid (apple cider or soy milk or
  evaporated or fresh milk)
1 egg
Whole wheat pie crust

Beat altogether in a large bowl or food processor and pour into a slightly prebaked 9-inch whole wheat pie crust. Bake at 425° for 15 minutes; reduce heat to 350° and bake for 35 minutes more, or until a knife inserted in the custard comes out clean.

Extra scrumptious with whipped cream and chopped toasted almonds.

Margaret Crenson

Apple Pie

2 c. flour
1 tsp. salt
2/3 c. margarine
5 to 7 T. ice water
6 lg. apples, peeled & sliced
  (Rome, Mac's, Granny Smith)

1/3+ c. brown sugar
1+ tsp. cinnamon
1/4 tsp. cloves
Margarine

Pie Crust: Mix together the flour and salt. With a fork or pastry blender, cut in the margarine until blended – dough should resemble peas. Mix in the ice water and blend until dough holds together. Divide dough in half. Turn 1/2 onto a floured board and roll to desired thickness and place into pie pan. Roll out second half and reserve for top.

Mix apples, spices and sugar. Pour into pan. Place on top crust and adjust to fit. Cut a few slits in the top crust and dot with margarine. Bake for 10 minutes at 450°. Then lower temperature to 350° and bake another 45 minutes.

C.R. Dill

Coconut-Buttermilk Pie

1 pie crust
2 c. flaked coconut
1/2 c. butter, melted
1 1/2 c. sugar
2 T. all-purpose flour

4 lg. eggs, beaten
1/2 c. buttermilk
1 tsp. vanilla extract
1 c. (6 oz.) semi-sweet chocolate
  morsels

Fit pie crust into a 9-inch pie plate. Bake at 450° for 5 minutes.

Toast coconut for 10 to 20 minutes at 325°, or until golden brown, stirring occasionally; set aside.

Beat sugar, butter and flour at medium speed until blended; add eggs, buttermilk and vanilla, beating well. Stir in toasted coconut and chocolate morsels. Pour into prepared pie crust. Bake at 325° for 30 minutes, shielding edges with foil to prevent excessive browning. Bake 25 to 30 minutes more, until set. Yield: 1 pie.

Variations: Try a graham cracker crust. To cut richness, use 1/2 cup chocolate morsels instead of 1 cup; add 1 to 2 fresh grated pears, it will still be delicious.   ***Kirsten Holm Schamberg***

Very Berry Cobbler

2 pt. raspberries or blackberries
1 1/2 pt. blueberries
1/3 c. + 1 tsp. sugar
2 1/2 c. + 2 T. all-purpose flour
2 T. freshly-squeezed lemon juice
Dash of ground cinnamon

1 tsp. salt
1/2 c. cold unsalted butter, cut into
  sm. pieces
1 lg. egg yolk
1 T. heavy cream

Heat oven to 400°. Place berries in a large bowl. Add 1/2 cup sugar, 2 tablespoons flour, lemon juice and cinnamon; toss to combine. Set aside.

To make the pâte brisée, place the remaining 2 1/2 cups flour, 1 teaspoon sugar and the salt in a food processor and process for a few seconds to combine. Add the butter; process until mixture resembles coarse meal, about 10 seconds. Add 1/4 cup ice water in a slow, steady stream through the feed tube with the machine running, just until the dough holds together. Do not process for more than 30 seconds. Turn dough out onto a piece of plastic wrap. Press into a flattened circle, and wrap it in the plastic; refrigerate for at least 1 hour.

On a lightly-floured surface, roll out the pastry into an 18-inch circle 1/8-inch thick. Fold the dough in half, and transfer to an 8 1/2 x 2 1/2-inch gratin dish or deep-dish pie plate. Carefully press the dough into the bottom and sides of the dish, allowing the excess to hang over the edge.

Spoon the berry mixture into the prepared dish, and fold the pastry in over the fruit. Trim away excess pastry, leaving an opening of about 3 inches in the center. Chill cobbler in the refrigerator until dough is firm, about 15 to 20 minutes.

Combine the egg yolk and cream in small bowl. Brush on top and bake about 30 minutes, until crust is golden. Reduce heat to 350°. Continue baking until juices start to bubble up over the crust, about 35 minutes more. Remove from oven, cool slightly and serve. Yield: 8 servings.

Ellen O'Shea

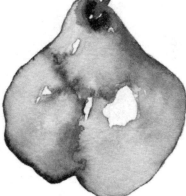

♥ Poached Pears with Spicy Wine Sauce

2 c. red wine
1 c. sugar
1 c. apple cider
1" to 2" long piece ginger root (I peeled it & cut into lg. chunks)
2 strips lemon peel (I made the strips as long as I could with my peeler)

3 to 5 black peppercorns
6 med.-sized firm, ripe Bosc or Bartlett pears
1/3 c. chopped pistachios or almonds
Mint leaves, for garnish

Start 2 hours before serving: Put wine, sugar, cider, ginger, lemon and peppercorns in 6-quart saucepan or Dutch oven.

Peel pears, leaving stem intact. With apple corer, core pears from bottoms. Place in wine mixture as they are peeled, turning to coat completely. Over high heat, heat to boiling. Reduce heat to low. Cover and simmer 30 to 45 minutes, or until easily pierced, turning pears after 15 minutes. With slotted spoon, remove pears.

Strain wine mixture, then return to saucepot. Over high heat, heat to boiling. Boil, uncovered, about 15 minutes, or until mixture reduces in volume and becomes syrupy.

To serve, spoon some syrup around pears. Sprinkle with nuts. Garnish each pear with a mint leaf. Yield: 6 servings.

From "Good Housekeeping", May 1992.

Nutritional Information per Serving: 280 calories, 4 gm fat, 5 mg sodium, 0 mg cholesterol.

Ed Berkel

Apple Pizza

Juice of 1/2 lemon
1 bag pizza dough (or homemade
  for 1 pizza)

3 Granny Smith apples
1/3 c. sugar
1 tsp. cinnamon

PIZZA DOUGH:
2 pkg. yeast
1 1/4 c. lukewarm water
3 1/2 c. flour

1 tsp. salt
1/4 c. olive oil
Pinch of sugar

TOPPING:
1 c. flour

1/2 to 3/4 c. sugar
1/4 c. melted butter

Pizza Dough: Mix yeast with water. Add flour, salt, olive oil and sugar. Let rise for 1 1/2 hours.

Spread dough out on round or rectangular pizza pan. Peel, slice and core apples. Add lemon juice, cinnamon and sugar to apples. Mix flour, sugar and melted butter; make crumbly, using fork or fingers. Spread apples on top of dough. Sprinkle topping on apples. Bake at 400° for about 15 to 20 minutes.

Clark Kelly

Hot Fudge Sauce

1 c. (6 oz.) chocolate chips
1 (14 oz.) can sweetened
  condensed milk (not evaporated
  milk)

2 T. butter
2 T. water
1 tsp. vanilla extract

In a medium-sized heavy saucepan over medium heat, melt chips with condensed milk, butter and water. Beat smooth with wire whisk if necessary. Stir in vanilla. Serve warm over ice cream or as a fruit dipping sauce. Store leftovers in refrigerator and reheat to serve. Yield: 2 cups.

Ann Smith

118

Too Good Fudge

My mother's fudge recipe was to die for, except that by the time you were done cooking it, stirring constantly to the crack stage (approximately 1 hour), and beating it until stiff (another 30 to 45 minutes), your arms certainly felt dead. Time and families march on, so I adapted this old recipe for the millennium. It really is too easy and too good.

I use a 2-cup Pyrex measuring cup that leaves only one item and utensils to clean up. In whatever microwave-safe dish you choose, place 1 cup confectioners' sugar, 2 tablespoons cocoa, 2 tablespoons butter (cold) and 1 tablespoon milk. Don't bother mixing, the microwave will do most of that. Microwave on HIGH for 1 minute, stir well at 30 seconds and finish microwaving. Remove from the microwave, if you have opened the door fast enough (I'm usually standing there waiting for mine), you will see a bubbly chocolate almost liquid, with the ingredients all combined. Add a dash of vanilla (about 1 teaspoon), a pinch of salt (about 1/4 teaspoon) and a good-sized glob of peanut butter. Mix it up. Mothers will recognize glob as the amount of peanut butter required for a peanut butter and jelly sandwich. The rest of you will have to improvise.

Butter a plate because as soon as it's mixed, pour it on the plate and press it out with your fingers to the desired thickness.

My mother insists pressing it out with your fingers is essential. That's how you add the love. You can eat it cold, but ours never lasts that long.

Adapted from an old family recipe by **Nancy Yu**.

Sinful Saltines

2 sticks butter	1 (12 oz.) bag chocolate chips
1/2 c. sugar	Chopped nuts
Saltines	

Cover a jellyroll pan with foil. Cover foil with saltines. Melt 2 sticks butter and 1/2 cup sugar. Bring to a full boil. Pour over saltines. Bake 10 minutes in preheated 350° oven. Remove from oven. Sprinkle chocolate chips over all and spread with the back of a spoon. Sprinkle with chopped nuts. Refrigerate until cool. Break into pieces. Keep refrigerated in a covered container.

Delicious!

Frances Catalano

Chocolate-Covered Pretzels

Solid chocolate   **Pretzels**

For this recipe, you can use any kind of chocolate you like (I like to use semi-sweet baking chocolate.) Put the chocolate into a microwave-safe bowl and put it into the microwave. Cook it for 1 minute on HIGH, then stir it and put it in for another 30 seconds (unless it is already melted). If it is still not melted, put it in for another 30 seconds, just make sure it doesn't burn! Next, set up a plate covered with waxed paper, cover the pretzels both front and back with chocolate. Put the pretzels on the waxed paper (as many as you want). Put into the refrigerator and wait until the chocolate hardens (it's faster in the freezer). Enjoy!   ***Marisa***

Susan Long's Nine-Layer Cookie Bars

1 stick butter, melted	1 c. coconut
1 tsp. vanilla	1 (6 oz.) pkg. white chocolate chips
1 c. graham cracker crumbs	1 can Eagle Brand sweetened
1 (6 oz.) pkg. chocolate chips	condensed milk
1 (6 oz.) pkg. butterscotch chips	1 c. chopped pecans

Layer each ingredient in a 9x13-inch baking dish, starting with the butter and ending with the pecans. Bake at 325° for 30 minutes.

♥ Banana Candle
(For Kids)

1 banana, for each candle	1 maraschino cherry,
2 pineapple slices (rings), for	for each candle
each candle	

Stack the pineapple rings in a shallow bowl or saucer. Cut the banana about 2/3 long. Insert the banana into the pineapple rings and notch the top to make a candle. Put the maraschino cherry on the banana to be the flame. Cut the banana slice and use it to make a handle for the candleholder.

Happy memories of eating these "candles" with my sister and brother when I was a child, and of watching my own children enjoy them.

Ann Nihal

This & That

Nestor Madalengoitia
First Harvest
Acrylic on 16 Canvases

How to Dry Flowers in a Microwave Oven

- You can preserve memories in minutes. Those flower garden favorites and party corsages will last for years if you dry them in a microwave oven. Pick sunflowers, marigolds, roses and other blooms while they are fresh.

- Thick-petaled flowers more easily retain their original shapes. Also flowers with thick centers are harder to dry. If you are in doubt, try a sample and judge for yourself.

- Bury the blossom in a silica gel or in a cornmeal-Borax mixture. Granular gel is available from hobby and flower shops. These substances can be reused after they have cooled.

- Pour a layer of drying base into a glass cup or pan. Cut flowers, leaving a 1/2-inch stem. Place stem down in drying material so blooms will not touch each other.

- Sprinkle more drying material over flowers - using a toothpick to spread petals to evenly fill space in between. Bury flowers completely.

- To dry a corsage, remove all wires and separate flowers.

- Most flowers need to be cooked from 1 to 2 minutes, roses 1 1/2 minutes, sunflowers 1 3/4 minutes. It depends on size. When done, the flower should be dry and firm. If it is soft or moist, it needs more cooking.

- Heat buried flowers by placing uncovered container in microwave oven. Set a cup of water in a glass in one corner of the oven. After cooking, allow to cool 10 to 15 minutes before uncovering. This time varies, too; roses need to stand 2 to 5 minutes. Sunflowers, however, should be left buried in their container in a plastic bag for 1 to 1 1/2 days.

- After this waiting period, slowly pour off drying material. Remove flowers and, working gently, pick off drying grains.

- You can recreate stems with wire and florist's tape. Leaves can be dried, too, using the same process.

This & That

Ball's Blue Book Apple-Maple Jam

3 qt. chopped, peeled, cored
   apples (about 6 lb.)
6 c. sugar
1 tsp. cinnamon

1/2 tsp. allspice
1/2 tsp. nutmeg
1/4 tsp. cloves
1 c. maple syrup

Combine all ingredients in a large saucepan. Bring slowly to a boil. Cook rapidly to gelling point. As mixture thickens, stir frequently to prevent sticking. Ladle hot jam into hot (sterilized) jars, leaving 1/4-inch headspace. Adjust 2-piece caps. Process 10 minutes in a boiling water canner. Yield: about 8 (half-pints).

Anonymous

♥ Fruit Shake

1 to 1 1/2 c. orange juice or
   pineapple juice
1 med. banana
3/4 c. blueberries, strawberries,
   raspberries or peaches (pick
   one of the above)

Blend juice of choice, banana and fruit of choice in a blender until smooth. Serve for breakfast or on a hot summers day.

Nancy McKenna

♥ Banana-Berry Batido

2 med. frozen, peeled
  bananas, sliced
1 T. honey

1 c. frozen blueberries or other
  berries of choice
2 c. calcium-fortified vanilla soy
  milk

Place all ingredients in a blender. Blend on low speed for 30 seconds, then on high speed for 30 seconds longer, or until smooth. Serve in chilled glasses. Yield: 4 servings, each with 100 calories.

Joanne Vanderveer

♥ Vegetable Pickles

Since this is not a vacuum-sealed canning project, keep these pickles refrigerated. They'll keep well for a week or more.

MARINADE:
1/2 c. apple cider vinegar
1/2 c. apple juice
1 tsp. salt

1 T. granulated sugar
2 cloves garlic, minced (opt.)
1 tsp. dill seed (opt.)

Choose any from among the following (it's appealing to combine 3 or 4 different vegetables) for a total of 4 cups:

Baby carrots
Broccoli florets, small bite-
  sized pieces
Cauliflower florets, small bite-
  size pieces
Green beans, trimmed & cut
  in half
Zucchini, sliced into 1/4"-thick
  rounds or into spears

Cucumbers, cut into spears,
  seeds trimmed if desired
  (small Kirby cucumbers are
  especially good for this)
Turnips, cut into short sticks
Celery, cut into short sticks
Red bell peppers, cut into strips

Combine the marinade ingredients with 1 cup water in a saucepan. Heat, stirring occasionally, until the salt and sugar are dissolved. Stir the vegetables you choose together and place them in a clean 1-quart jar. Pour the hot marinade over them. Cover tightly with lid and refrigerate for about 24 hours before serving. Yield: 2 quarts.

Adapted from "The Vegetarian Family Cookbook" by **Nava Atlas**.

♥ Perfect Dried Basil

Harvest your basil on a sunny morning. Remove the leaves, being careful to check for insects. (They would rather not be involved in the process.) If you wash it, make sure it's dry before proceeding.

From a roll of plain white paper toweling, tear off two connected sheets at a time. On each double sheet, place a single layer of basil leaves, close together, allowing an inch of space around the edges of the toweling. Then roll up and secure the ends with twist ties or elastics, so that it looks like a child's party favor. Place the rolls in an unused space in the refrigerator (not in a plastic bag) and check in a couple of weeks – it might take longer – to see if the leaves have dried.

When they have dried, put them in the food processor and chop until they are fine enough to sprinkle in your recipes. Store in tightly closed jars and enjoy all winter, remembering the summertime......

This fool-proof method came to me indirectly from Jean Alese, whom I consider a friend though I never met her! The leaves stay green and aromatic, unlike other methods I've tried, and I hope that you, too, will find it wonderful.

Margaret Crenson

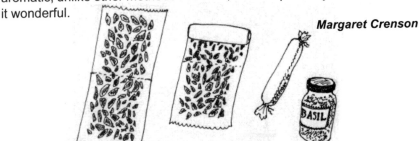

Charlotte Hires' Scramble

A trail mix of sorts.

2 lb. mixed nuts
1 bag Bugles
1 sm. box bite-size Shredded
   Wheat
1 pkg. Pepperidge Farm
   Goldfish
1 pkg. pretzels (small rings
   work well)
1 sm. box Cheerios
2 T. Worcestershire sauce
1 T. garlic salt
1 T. Jane's Crazy mixed-up salt
1 c. canola or safflower oil

Mix all dry ingredients in large bowl. Mix wet ingredients in separate bowl, then add to the dry ingredients. Mix well. Spread in a large, flat pan, such as a roasting pan. Bake at 250° for 2 hours, shaking the pan every 15 minutes. Yield: 2 gallons.

Herb Vinegars

One cup of fresh herbs will flavor 1 quart of vinegar. If you are using fresh herbs from the garden, cut them in the morning, rinse and gently pat dry with a towel. You can use an herb that's flowering. It will be milder but prettier! Use a good quality vinegar. I suggest trying a champagne vinegar or you can use wine vinegars, apple cider vinegar or, of course, plain vinegar. Use any clean glass bottle or jar with a tight-fitting lid or cork. You can recycle wine or oil bottles if you'd like, just make sure they are thoroughly cleaned. Gently place the herbs loosely in the bottle, fill with vinegar making sure herbs are totally submerged, cap and label, and put in a cool dark place for 3 to 4 weeks. After a few days, check and make sure the herbs are still covered (you might need to add more vinegar). It's as simple as that! The vinegar will stay fresh for about a year and can be used on salads or steamed vegetables, in sauces or as marinades for fish, poultry or meat.

Here are a few combinations you can try: put chives and a few chive blossoms in a light pink champagne vinegar with a garlic clove or two. Fill with dill and a blossom in white wine vinegar, or a few sprigs of tarragon and a peeled shallot.

Other suggestions are: equal amounts of rosemary and lemon thyme, basil with a couple cloves of garlic, coriander and oregano with garlic and a dried red chili pepper. You get the idea...have fun!!

Claudia Gorman

♥ Dog Cookies

2 c. wheat or white flour
2/3 c. yellow cornmeal
1/2 c. shelled sunflower seeds
2 T. corn/canola oil

1/2 c. chicken broth
2 eggs, mixed with 1/4 c. low-fat
  milk
1 egg, beaten

Preheat oven to 350°. In large bowl, mix together flour, cornmeal and seeds. Add oil, broth and egg mix. Dough should be firm. Let set 15 minutes. On a lightly-floured surface, roll dough out 1/4-inch thick. Cut into desired shapes and brush with beaten egg on cookie sheet. Bake for 25 minutes, or so, until golden brown. Remove from sheet and cool. Store in airtight container. Yield: 45 to 60 cookies.

K. Preyer

Feed the Birds

Modified from the Nature Museum Cookbook.

Once you start feeding the birds in the winter, be sure to continue it regularly. When birds find food in one place they will return to it. Not all birds like the same food, so a variety is good. Seeds, cracked corn, suet, peanut butter, cooking fats, heads of sunflower seeds, sprigs of berries, sliced fruit, sprigs of rose hips and halves of coconut are all good.

Suet Food Mix: Use hardened white fat leftover from cooking steaks on broiler pan. Mix with sunflower seeds and mixed bird seed. Place on edge of feeder or place in stander suet feeder.

Bird lovers know to feed birds suet in winter. Few realize this to be a no, no during warm months. Birds can die from eating suet (the waxy fat from beef) in warm months, especially in summer. Their metabolic system cannot take it! But in winter, suet can save birds from dying on cold winter days when no other food is available.

Pine Cone Feeder: Use large pine cone and fill open spaces with mix of peanut butter and mixed bird seed. Use equal parts. Hang pine cone on branch.

Chickadee Pudding: Mix a handful of dry rolled oats, a handful of bird seed, a handful of cornmeal, a handful of ground bread crumbs, a spoonful of peanut butter, a handful cut-up raisins, a handful of Cream of Wheat, and enough bacon grease or fat leftover from cooking steaks in a pan to moisten. Put in feeder, on large pine cone, or tin pie plate.

Birds Christmas Tree: Decorate a tree or shrub for the birds. Hang pine cones covered with bird pudding. Make orange and grapefruit cups filled with seeds. Hang slices of orange and grapefruits, chunks of suet and chunks of coconut. Then decorate with sprigs of berries. String garlands of popcorn and cranberries to go around the tree. You'll love it, and so will the birds.

Food to make birds eat out of your hand: Dedicated bird lovers have discovered that live mealworms can literally entice birds to eat out of their hands! Mealworms can be tossed on the ground, near a bird feeder, and with patience and time, the birds can be lured to accept worms from a container in your hand. Patience and love for the bird is the key! They are available from most good pet stores and/or you can raise your own. Mealworms are the larvae of a beetle, Tenebrio moliroe, a common pest of flour, grain and meal.

Come feed the little birds
Show them you care
And you'll be glad if you do,
Their young ones are hungry,
Their nests are so bare
All it takes is tup-pence from you

"Feed The Birds" from Mary Poppins

Restaurants
and Professional Chefs

Doug Nobiletti
Harmony of the Pans
Copernicus Says So. #1 Series 1
Digital Photography

Equivalent Measurements

3 tsp.	1 Tbsp.	2 cups	1 pt.
4 Tbsp.	1/4 cup	4 cups	1 qt.
5 1/3 Tbsp.	1/3 cup	4 qt.	1 gal.
8 Tbsp.	1/2 cup	8 qt.	1 peck
10 2/3 Tbsp.	2/3 cup	4 pecks	1 bu.
12 Tbsp.	3/4 cup	16 oz.	1 lb.
16 Tbsp.	1 cup	32 oz.	1 qt.
1/2 cup	1 gill	8 oz. liquid	1 cup
		1 oz. liquid	2 Tbsp.

(For liquid and dry measurements use standard measuring spoons and cups. All measurements are level.)

Ingredient Measurements

Baking powder
1 cup = 5 1/2 oz.

Cheese, American
1 lb. = 2 2/3 cups cubed

Cocoa
1 lb. = 4 cups ground

Coffee
1 lb. = 5 cups ground

Cornmeal
1 lb. = 3 cups

Cornstarch
1 lb. = 3 cups

Cracker crumbs
23 soda crackers = 1 cup
15 graham crackers = 1 cup

Shortening or Butter
1 lb. = 2 cups

Eggs
1 egg = 4 Tbsp. liquid
4 to 5 whole = 1 cup
7 to 9 whites = 1 cup
12 to 14 yolks = 1 cup

Flour
1 lb. all-purpose = 4 cups
1 lb. cake = 4 1/2 cups
1 lb. graham = 3 1/2 cups

Lemons, juice
1 medium = 2 to 3 Tbsp.
5 to 8 medium = 1 cup

Lemons, rind
1 lemon = 1 Tbsp. grated

Oranges, juice
1 medium = 2 to 3 Tbsp.
3 to 4 medium = 1 cup

Oranges, rind
1 = 2 Tbsp. grated

Gelatin
3 1/4 oz. pkg. flavored
= 1/2 cup
1/4 oz. pkg. unflavored
= 1 Tbsp.

Sugar
1 lb. brown = 2 1/2 cups
1 lb. cube = 96 to 160 cubes
1 lb. granulated = 2 cups
1 lb. powdered = 3 1/2 cups

Restaurants and Professional Chefs

"Imagination is more important than knowledge."
Albert Einstein

Cubano Grilled Panini
Demitasse Café
Poughkeepsie, NY

1 1/2 oz. thin sliced pork
1 1/2 oz. thin sliced Virginia ham
4 sliced pickles
2 slices Swiss cheese
A few spinach leaves

2 oz. mustard
2 oz. roasted garlic spread (see recipe)
2 slices ciabatta bread (sold fresh at most bakeries)

Spread mustard on 1 slice of cibatta bread. Place pickles on top. Spread garlic spread on other half. Arrange pork, ham, Swiss cheese, spinach, and put sandwich together. Place on panini press for 4 to 5 minutes and serve.

If you don't have a panini press, you can cook it in a frying pan like you would make grilled cheese.

Roasted Garlic Spread
Demitasse Café
Poughkeepsie, NY

1 head garlic
Mayonnaise

Olive oil

Preheat oven to 350°. Remove loose papery skin from head of garlic. Cut off the tips of the cloves. Coat with olive oil (just a little) and wrap it in tinfoil. After about 1/2 hour, check the garlic for doneness. The cloves should be very soft to the touch. It will probably take about 45 minutes, depending on the size of the head of garlic. Let cool.

In each clove, you will find garlic paste. Mix 4 cloves to 1 cup mayonnaise to make roasted garlic spread.

Roasted garlic is tasty and mild, you can spread it on a piece of bread instead of butter.

Frigo Zucchini Sticks

Coppola's Poughkeepsie
Jim Morgan

2 zucchini squash, rinsed   **Flour**
Salt

On a medium-sized cutting board, cut off top and bottom of squash. Then cut zucchini into equal thirds. If the squash is a medium-large size, cut it into equal 1/4's. Then take each 1/4, stand it up and slice downward, making approximately 1/4-inch slices. Once slices are made, lay them down flat and one at a time, make julienne sticks. Repeat and be sure all are separated. Place zucchini sticks in a deep kitchen bowl. Sprinkle fairly liberally with salt and tenderly toss with your hands. This salt and hand action will release all the water in the vegetable. Strain well. Let rest for 10 to 15 minutes for best results. Then take a bowl and put flour on side. Put sticks in the strainer. Hold strainer over bowl to receive shaken flour. Cover zucchini with a lot of flour, shaking it back and forth to coat each piece with flour. Keep repeating a couple of times until a nice coating is on all of the sticks. The excess flour should be all shaken off now. Tip the contents into the basket of deep fryer. The temperature should be set at 375°. Drop basket in hot oil; take a kitchen fork to keep them from sticking together, and move them around, about 2 to 3 minutes, until golden, in fryer, then remove and tip onto dish with a paper towel. Plate and serve immediately.

Jalapeño Hush Puppies
Spanky's Restaurant
Poughkeepsie, NY

2 c. yellow cornmeal
1 c. all-purpose flour
2 whole eggs
1 c. milk or buttermilk
1 fresh jalapeño, finely chopped

2 scallions, finely chopped
1/2 red onion, finely chopped
1 tsp. salt
1/4 tsp. cayenne pepper
1/2 tsp. baking powder

Combine dry ingredients in medium bowl. In a separate bowl, mix eggs and milk, then rest of ingredients. Pour wet mix over dry, mixing thoroughly. Heat 2 inches vegetable (canola or peanut) oil in a large heavy saucepot until thermometer reaches 300°. Carefully drop rounded spoonfuls of batter into oil and fry until golden brown, about 4 to 5 minutes. Remove and drain on paper towel. Serve with your favorite tartar sauce or ranch dip. Yield: about 12 (2-inch) round balls.

♥ Scallops and Black Pepper with Mint Basil Yogurt Sauce

Fig
Poughkeepsie, NY

MINT-BASIL YOGURT SAUCE:
3/4 c. whole milk yogurt
1 clove garlic, minced
1 T. chopped fresh mint
1 T. chopped fresh basil
1/2 tsp. ground coriander
1/2 tsp. ground cumin
Salt, to taste

SCALLOPS:
2 T. freshly-ground pepper
18 sea scallops (preferably Divers)
1 T. vegetable oil
Salt

36 very fresh med.-sized basil leaves

Sauce: Combine all sauce ingredients and whisk together. Season to taste with salt. Refrigerate until you are ready to serve.

Scallops: Prepare scallops, place pepper on a plate. Season scallops with salt, then dredge them lightly on both sides in the pepper. Heat the vegetable oil in a large sauté pan over high heat until smoking. Place the scallops in pan, cook for about 1 minute per side. Cut them in half so you have 2 half circles.

To serve, place a little of the sauce in a basil leaf, place one of the scallop halves on it and drizzle a little extra sauce over it. Serve immediately. Yield: 6 servings as an appetizer.

Fig's Roasted Vegetables on Garlic Croustade

Fig
Poughkeepsie, NY

3 med. zucchini
1 med. eggplant
1/2 lb. mushrooms
2 med. onions
3 red bell peppers
1 baguette

1/3 c. olive oil
Salt & pepper, to taste
1 T. dry basil
1/4 c. balsamic vinegar
3 T. finely-chopped curly parsley

Wash all vegetables. Salt eggplant on both sides to remove bitterness for 15 minutes. Rinse and squeeze eggplant. Dice and toss zucchini, eggplant, mushrooms and onions with oil. Put vegetables on a cookie sheet in a single layer, and roast in a 400° oven for 30 to 40 minutes. Stir every 15 minutes.

Meanwhile, roast red peppers separately on stove-top burner. Put peppers in a bowl together and cover with plastic wrap until cooled. Then rub off charred skin. Dice and add to the other vegetables. Add basil, vinegar and parsley. Add salt and pepper to taste. Cut baguette into 1/2-inch slices.

Heat pan, add half of the olive oil and half of the crushed garlic. Line pan with 1 layer of sliced baguette. Grill until golden, turn and grill the other side a minute or two more. Make several batches. Spoon roasted vegetables onto garlic croustade and serve promptly. Yield: 25 to 30 pieces.

Note: Vegetables can be made up to 2 days ahead. In fact, this allows the flavors to meld and deepen.

Pickwick Veal

Dicken's Restaurant
James Roth, Executive Chef
Poughkeepsie, NY

2 lb. veal cutlets (2 to 3 oz. per
   cutlet)
1/4 c. flour
4 eggs
1/4 c. milk
1/8 c. Parmesan cheese, grated
Salt & pepper, to taste

2 T. shallots, minced
2 T. garlic, minced
1/2 c. sun-dried tomatoes, julienned
1/4 lb. button mushrooms
1 1/2 c. port wine
1/4 lb. butter
1/4 c. Pommace olive oil

Pound out veal until thin. Combine eggs, milk, cheese, salt and pepper; whip together. Heat sauté pan and add oil. Dredge veal in flour, then in egg mixture and sauté until browned on both sides. Remove from pan and keep warm in oven. To the pan, add shallots, garlic, sun-dried tomatoes and mushrooms; sauté for 1 minute. Add port wine; reduce until about 1/4 cup left, turn off heat. Add butter, stirring constantly, making sure it does not separate. Place veal on plates and top with sauce.

When cooking with wine, always leave the pan uncovered as you cook. The allows the alcohol to burn off and results in liquid with a rounder, fruitier flavor.

Ruby Shallot Chicken with Emerald City Rice

Amie
Tamara Champion
Fishkill, NY

4 thin chicken breasts
2 cloves garlic, crushed
1/2 lemon, juiced
1 tsp. kosher salt
8 shallots, thinly sliced

1 1/2 c. ruby port
1/4 c. chilled butter cubes
4 fresh sage leaves
Salt & pepper, to taste
Extra-virgin olive oil, for sauté

RICE:
2 c. water
1 c. canilla rice
1/2 tsp. salt
1 T. extra-virgin olive oil
1 c. fresh parsley leaves

4 fresh sage leaves
1 T. fresh rosemary leaves
1 T. fresh thyme leaves
1 clove garlic
1/8 c. extra-virgin olive oil
Salt & pepper, to taste

Marinate chicken breasts in garlic, lemon juice and salt for 1 hour. Sauté chicken breast on high heat in large sauté pan until cooked through (remove from pan). Sauté shallots until they are tender. Add ruby port to deglaze pan (reduce by half). Mount port/shallot reduction with butter to create a beautifully ruby sauce. Add sage leaves just before serving. Salt and pepper to taste. Submerge chicken in sauce to heat for serving.

Rice: Boil water, salt and olive oil over high heat. Add rice, bring back to a boil, then reduce to simmer, covered, for approximately 20 minutes.

In food processor, combine parsley, sage, rosemary, thyme, garlic, olive oil, salt and pepper to create an emerald green pesto. Fold pesto into cooked rice.

Plating: Spoon approximately 1/2 cup Emerald City rice onto center of plate. Place 1 chicken breast atop rice. Spoon ruby shallot sauce atop chicken. Garnish with 1 of the sage leaves from the sauce. Enjoy! Yield: 4 servings.

Shrimp Diane
Spanky's Restaurant
Poughkeepsie, NY

1/2 c. minced shallots	1 T. Dijon mustard
1 T. cracked peppercorns	2 c. heavy cream
2 c. sliced mushrooms, fresh	1 tsp. dry tarragon
1 lb. (16 to 20 count) shrimp, raw, peeled & cleaned	1 lb. penne pasta (or any other bite-sized), cooked al dente &
2 oz. brandy	drained

Over medium-high heat, add 1 tablespoon oil or butter and shallots, peppercorns, mushrooms and shrimp. When shrimp begin to cook (turn pink), remove pan from heat and add brandy. Carefully put pan back on stove (it may flame up). Add heavy cream, mustard and tarragon, stirring to combine. Reduce cream by about half and add pasta. Toss to coat. Yield: 3 to 4 servings.

Baked Ziti Siciliano
Villa Marissa
Michael DeSantis
Poughkeepsie, NY

1/2 lb. ziti	8 oz. ricotta cheese
1 sm. eggplant	4 oz. Romano cheese
1 qt. tomato sauce	4 oz. shredded Mozzarella cheese
2 eggs	1 c. flour
Seasoned bread crumbs	Salt, for boiling water

Preheat oven to 375°. Cook ziti in water with 1/2 tablespoon salt, to desired tenderness. Cool with cold water. Skin your eggplant and slice 1/4-inch slices. Flour, egg and bread the eggplant. Brush with oil. Bake in oven at 375° for 20 minutes, or until golden brown and tender (set aside).

In a bowl, put 3/4 of your tomato sauce, also place in ricotta cheese, Romano cheese and Mozzarella cheese. Mix with a spoon until all is blended. Add in your cooled ziti; mix together and set aside.

In your baking pan, put in remaining sauce and 1/8 cup water. Place in your baked ziti mixture and then chop up your eggplant. Place it on top of the baked ziti. Place in oven at 375° for 15 to 20 minutes, until golden brown. Top with Mozzarella cheese for 5 minutes of cook time. Yield: dinner for 2.

Bolognese Sauce

Beech Tree Grill
Poughkeepsie, NY

1/2 lb. ground lamb
1/2 lb. ground beef
1/2 lb. ground pork
1 1/2 c. chopped onion
2 T. chopped garlic
1/4 bunch fresh thyme, picked
   from stem

2 c. red wine
32 oz. chopped tomatoes (canned
   will do)
2 1/2 T. extra-virgin olive oil
Salt & pepper, to taste

Sauté onions and garlic in olive oil until softened. Brown meat in 2-quart stock-pot. Add red wine to meat and simmer until wine is reduced by half. Add chopped tomatoes, sautéed garlic and onions, and picked thyme. Simmer slowly for 1 hour. Stir often. Season with salt and pepper. Toss with your favorite pasta, grated Pecorino Romano and enjoy!

Coconut Pineapple Ice Cream in Graham Cracker-White Chocolate Shell

Michael Rozman, Chef of
The Haymaker
Poughkeepsie, NY

ICE CREAM:
1 qt. heavy cream
12 egg yolks
1 c. sugar (granulated)
1 ripe pineapple

1/4 c. Malibu coconut rum
1/4 c. coconut milk
1 tsp. Coco Lopez
1 T. Mascarpone cheese
1 Madagascar bourbon vanilla bean

SHELL:
2 c. crumbled graham crackers
1/2 c. melted unsalted butter

1/8 c. sugar (granulated)
1/4 lb. white chocolate, shaved

GARNISH:
Toasted coconut or fresh blueberry

Place a saucepot on a medium flame, filled with water to boil. Separate 12 egg yolks into a metal mixing bowl. Add sugar; mix.

In another saucepot, put heavy cream, coconut milk, vanilla bean and coconut rum. Bring to a boil, then turn off. Slowly add the cream mixture (while hot) to the egg yolks while mixing thoroughly with a wooden spoon. Add Coco Lopez and Mascarpone to mixture. Place over pot with boiling water (double boiler) and stir continuously while cooking. After about 7 minutes the mixture should start to thicken. Strain and let cool completely (3 hours in a refrigerator). Add to your ice cream machine and freeze.

Shell: Preheat oven to 400˚. Melt butter. Mix graham cracker crumbs and sugar. Add melted butter and combine. Form mixture into the cupcake tins and bake in your oven for about 10 to 12 minutes (or until toasted). Remove and sprinkle shaved white chocolate evenly over warm shells. Let cool completely.

Once ice cream is almost frozen, fold in pineapple (small diced) and place in a piping bag with a large rose tip. Pipe into the shells evenly and freeze overnight. Once frozen, you may flip the dessert out of the tin and you may garnish with toasted coconut or fresh fruit (blueberries are good – optional). Yield: 6 portions.

Brandy Peach Ring

Lou Strippoli
Caffe Aurora
Poughkeepsie, NY

STEP 1:
1 c. all-purpose flour
1 c. sugar
1 tsp. baking soda

1/4 tsp. salt
1/4 tsp. nutmeg
1/4 tsp. cinnamon

STEP 2:
1/2 c. vegetable oil
1 extra-lg. egg

1/2 tsp. vanilla extract
1 (15 oz.) can sliced peaches
4 oz. brandy (opt.)

Preheat oven to 350°. Spray a 9-inch bundt pan with Pam cooking spray release and sprinkle sugar to coat inside of pan, using sugar from step 1. In a large bowl, stir together flour, remaining sugar from step 1, salt, nutmeg and cinnamon. Next, add vegetable oil, egg and vanilla extract; mix together to form a paste. Drain peaches and add to mixture, then add brandy and pour into a bundt pan. Bake approximately 50 minutes to 1 hour, until cake springs back when lightly touched. Cool 1/2 hour and remove from pan into serving plate.

Excellent all by itself or garnish with additional peaches.

Vanilla Bean Crème Brûlée

Beech Tree Grill
Poughkeepsie, NY

1 qt. heavy cream (preferably 36% butterfat)
1 c. granulated sugar

1 vanilla bean
Pinch of salt
12 egg yolks

Preheat oven to 290°.

Mix heavy cream, 1/2 cup sugar and pinch of salt in saucepan. Split vanilla bean. Scrape inside paste into heavy cream mixture. Separate 12 eggs, keeping yolks in a large mixing bowl. Discard egg whites. Add remaining sugar to egg yolks. Set aside egg mixture. Place saucepan on low flame. Bring heavy cream mixture to rolling boil while stirring constantly. Once boiling, remove from heat. Slowly pour cream into egg yolks and remainder of sugar. Pour batter into 6 ramekins*. Place ramekins in a water bath (roasting pan filled 1/3 of the way with water will work nicely). Place in 290° oven for 45 minutes. Remove and cool completely before refrigerating. Crèmes will stay fresh up to 2 days in refrigerator. Yield: 6 servings.

Brûlée: At the time you wish to serve the crème, you must make the brûlée. First, pat moisture off the top of the crème with a paper towel. Sprinkle with granulated sugar, completely covering crème with a thin coat. Place ramekins under broiler until sugar topping becomes brown. (Or, you may use a baker's butane torch to brown sugar.) Remove from broiler and allow brûlée to cool and harden.

*Ramekins are ovenproof, single serving dishes.

Enjoy!

To prevent vanilla beans from drying out, place the beans in a small jar, add just enough rum to keep the tips of the beans wet, and cover securely. The beans will absorb a bit of the liquid and will not dry out with time.

Index

144

FAVORITE RECIPES
FROM MY COOKBOOK

Recipe Name	Page Number

Artist Credits

Barrett, Tom 46, 140, back of divider
Burda, Denise 85, 86
Cadore, Gene 78, 138
Carlson, Elma 45
Crenson, Dick 18, 21, 28, back cover
Crenson, Margaret 7, 13, 20, 79, 89, 112, 113, 123, 131, divider
Dill, Cynthia 11, 33, 60, 66, 76, 103, 125
Eby, Connye 26, 130
Gorman, Claudia 24, 29, 69, 90, 93, 94, 119, 124, divider
Johnson, Jeep 4, 27, 70, 139
Jordan, Jeannine 51
McGinnis, Kelly 74
McHugh, Marie-Louise 31, 34, 108
Madalengoitia, Nestor 23, divider
Maranto, H. Darlyne 72
Monte-Caruso, Theresa 24, 41, 121
Morse, Ann Lawrance 146
Nadel, Seth 16, divider
Nihal, Ann 6, 62, 83, 120, divider
Nobiletti, Doug 10, 40, 127, divider
O'Shea, Ellen Metzger 37, 38, 42, 53, 55, 81, 98, 115, 129, divider
Palaia, Franc 1, divider
Peckham, Jayne 100
Petruccio, Steven James 35, 48, 64, 91, 104, 121, 125, 133, 136
Ransome, James 67, cover, title page
Rein, Samuel 88, 116, 128, divider
Schamberg, Claes 59
Seaman, Elayne 110
Small, Helene divider
Spangler, Alec 82, 109
Suares, J.C. 43
Volk, Karl 56, 92
Watsky, Enid divider
Waxtel, Leslie 132
Wells, M.G. 9, 96, 106, 114
Willard, Nancy divider
Yu, Nancy 14
Zappelli, Carol 2

146

Thanks to all who helped to make this cookbook possible (and a huge thank-you to Doug Nobiletti for your time and expertise!).

These recipes are not Barrett Art Center creations; they are favorites of our contributors'. We, therefore, do not endorse or guarantee in any way their success or safety.

The Barrett Art Center is a funded member of the Dutchess County Arts Council.

Barrett Art Center
55 Noxon St., Poughkeepsie, NY 12601
(845) 471-2550 • www.barrettartcenter.org

ORDER BLANK

NAME _____

ADDRESS _____

CITY & STATE _____ ZIP _____

How many copies? _____   Amount enclosed _____
Price per book $14.95
Postage & handling 3.95
Total $18.90
Please make checks payable to:
                   Barrett Art Center
Mail orders to: Barrett Art Center Cookbook
                   55 Noxon St.
                   Poughkeepsie, NY 12601

        B.A.C. members receive a 10% discount

ORDER BLANK

NAME _____

ADDRESS _____

CITY & STATE _____ ZIP _____

How many copies? _____   Amount enclosed _____
Price per book $14.95
Postage & handling 3.95
Total $18.90
Please make checks payable to:
                   Barrett Art Center
Mail orders to: Barrett Art Center Cookbook
                   55 Noxon St.
                   Poughkeepsie, NY 12601

        B.A.C. members receive a 10% discount

EXCELLENT FUND-RAISING IDEAS

In addition to printing cookbooks for fund-raising organizations, JUMBO JACK'S COOKBOOKS also offers the proven successful fund-raising products shown below. The products shown below are just a few of the many items you might select for your next fund-raising project, or perhaps in conjunction with your cookbook project. Any of these will be beautifully imprinted with your organization's logo and name.

If you are interested in helping your organization make money with these successful fund-raising products, just mark the products you'd like more information about, and give us your name and address.

Name_____

Address _____

Phone _____

Tear out this page and mail it to: JUMBO JACK'S COOKBOOKS
P.O. 247 • AUDUBON, IOWA 50025

❏ OVEN MITT

❏ HOT PAD

❏ TOTE BAG

❏ APRON

❏ COOKBOOK

❏ T-SHIRT

❏ MUG

❏ PLACE MAT

Or, if you prefer, give Jeanne a toll free call at 1-800-798-2635, ext. 231
FAX: 1-712-563-3118 • COLLECT: 1-712-563-2635

We hope you are enjoying using this cookbook and find it useful in your kitchen. This book was printed by JUMBO JACK'S COOKBOOKS. If you are interested in having cookbooks printed for your organization, please write us for prices and details.

A cookbook is a good way for YOUR organization to make money.

If you are interested in more information, just tear out this page and mail it to us with your name and address, or just call us toll-free 1-800-798-2635.

UP TO 90 DAYS INTEREST FREE!

Featuring the 3-ring easel binder

We also do hardback covers, square back wire covers, and other types of binding.

Yes - please send me more information!

Name _____

Organization _____

Address _____

City _____ State _____ Zip _____

Phone _____

JUMBO JACK'S COOKBOOKS
AUDUBON MEDIA CORPORATION
AUDUBON IA 50025 • 1-800-798-2635